LIFE
ANSWERS
Making Sense of Your World

TONY BEAM
& ALEX McFARLAND

FOREWORD BY JOSH McDOWELL

Auxano
PRESS

ISBN: 978-0-9973414-8-5

Published by Auxano Press, Traveler's Rest, South Carolina. www.AuxanoPress.com.

Page Design and Layout: Josh Hunt

Cover design: CrosslinCreative.net

Cover Image: iStock.com

Editorial and Project Management: Maleah Bell

Printed in the United States of America

18 19 20 21 22 23—6 5 4 3 2 1

Dedication

I would like to dedicate the book to all former, current, and future members of the Life Answers Team at North Greenville University, and to Ms. Robin McCarter, whose tireless work and dedication holds the Christian Worldview Center together.

Tony Beam

My portions of this book are dedicated to the wonderful family that is North Greenville University, and especially to my colleagues Dr. Tony Beam and Ms. Robin McCarter. Dr. Beam's vision for our Life Answers Team is a prime example of putting apologetics/worldview content to practical use in the spirit of 1 Peter 3:15; Ephesians 4:11–12; and John 17:21, "that the world may believe."

Alex McFarland

Contents

Acknowledgments

I want to thank my sweet and supportive wife, Denise, for allowing me to sacrifice some of our time so I would have the time necessary to make this book a reality.

I also want to thank my dear friends and colleagues, Alex McFarland, director of the Christian Worldview Center; Dr. Ken Hemphill; and all of the administrative team at North Greenville University for their support for this project.

My thanks go to the late Chuck Colson, whose book *How Now Shall We Live* made me passionate about apologetics and inspired me to begin the Christian Worldview Center in 2004 at North Greenville University.

Finally, I want to thank the South Carolina Christian Foundation for believing in this project enough to invest their financial resources. This book would not have been published without their generous financial support.

Tony Beam

A project of this scope is made possible by the contributions of many gracious people.

I am thankful to apologetics legend Josh McDowell, who has influenced my life so incredibly (and who also graciously wrote our Foreword).

I would like to thank Dr. Ken Hemphill for inviting Dr. Beam and myself to write for Auxano; this is a great honor, as I have respected Dr. Hemphill and followed his ministry for years.

I am thankful to Dillon Burroughs, my longtime friend, colleague, and research assistant for his contributions.

I am indebted to Rev. Bert Harper, my co-host on "Exploring the Word"; Jim Stanley of American Family Radio; and Tim Wildmon, president of the American Family Association—all of whom encourage me and graciously promote my books.

For Ms. Leslie Brown, research librarian at North Greenville University, who truly is "queen of even the most elusive footnotes."

For my wife, Angie, who has been patiently proofreading my writing for more than twenty-five years, I am so grateful!

Most of all, I am thankful for the Lord Jesus Christ, who loved me and gave Himself for me.

Alex McFarland

Foreword

The Word of God tells us in 1 Peter 3:15 to "always be prepared to give an answer to everyone who asks you to give the reason for the hope that you have." Notice the words *answer* and *reason*. In the original language in which the New Testament was written, the word used gives us the term *apologetics*. As followers of Jesus Christ, we are commanded to be prepared to explain *what* we believe and the reasons *why* we believe.

This verse in 1 Peter concludes by reminding us that we are to share the Christian message "with gentleness and respect." The gospel is the greatest message in all of history! How much God loves us, how He sent His Son to die for our sins, how we may be forgiven and eternally secure in Christ's love—it all truly is "good news"! The New Testament call to apologetics tells us to present and defend the faith, but to always communicate ways that honor and reflect well on our Savior.

It is more important than ever that the church takes seriously this call. Years ago, when I wrote the first edition of *Evidence that Demands a Verdict*, who would have believed that by the dawn of the twenty-first century there would be such a cultural rejection of truth? In the 1990s and early 2000s some readers thought my books *The New Tolerance* and *The Last Christian Generation* were a little over the top, and perhaps "alarmist," about how dark the culture was becoming.

Yet people of all ages are still hungry to know who God is. Our world has become more aligned against God and His

Word than ever before. But if precious souls are to be won to eternal life, and if America's families are to be restored, the church must act now.

That's why I am so excited about the resource you hold in your hands, *Life Answers*, written by my friends Alex McFarland and Tony Beam. Alex has been a trusted ministry partner for years, and he and I have partnered together in many conferences, broadcasts, and outreach projects. Dr. Tony Beam is a vice president at North Greenville University, a leading Christian school in South Carolina. Alex and Tony share my passion to effectively show Jesus to the 80-million-strong generation known as "millennial" (and younger) to stand strong for the Christian faith. *Life Answers* lives up to its name! Alex and Tony are giving readers solid apologetics and Christian worldview content—with fresh research and relatable, real-life truth.

Josh

Josh McDowell
www.josh.org

Introduction

Apologetics...
What is it?
Why does the church need this today?
How is this relevant to me?

We live in a unique and exciting time in history. The recent explosion of new technologies has given birth to a world that is intricately connected. For those who love to travel, planes flying at near the speed of sound, a web of interstate highways, and high-speed trains that stretch the limits of passenger safety all transport people around the world. For those who do not wish to travel physically, the Internet makes virtual travel a reality by supplying all the pictures, videos, and information one can possibly want from any part of the world. Video chat applications have made it possible to talk face-to-face from anywhere on the planet. Pocket-sized global positioning systems make getting from point A to point B both exciting and efficient.

All of this technology has resulted in massive globalization. Eastern cultures are no longer unique to Eastern societies. The technologies of the twentieth and twenty-first centuries have revolutionized humanity. It is no longer uncommon for people to have friends scattered across the world.

What are the implications of all this globalizing technology? It is truly transforming that cultures are intertwining, making it possible to experience a variety of cultures without traveling far from home. However, globalization has also caused a greater awareness of other religions and belief systems. For example, Eastern religions broke into pop culture in the 1960s with bands like The Beatles and Earth, Wind, and Fire embracing and promoting them. Islam came to the forefront during the late 1970s with the American hostage situation in Iran; the first Gulf War in the early 1990s; and, more recently, the September 11, 2001 terrorist attacks, followed by the war on terror, which is ongoing. Atheist blogs are common on the Internet with social media sites serving as safe harbors for what are often extreme individual beliefs.

On the positive side, this globalization gives Christians a great opportunity to share Christ with the world. On the negative side, persons who are weak in their faith may begin to doubt once their beliefs are challenged by unfamiliar belief systems. This problem leads us to one of the core purposes for apologetics. *Apologetics* is simply a field of study that gives reasonable proof that a faith is true. Christian apologetics seeks to provide reasonable evidence against other belief systems that Christianity is true and reliable. For example, this book will examine important issues, such as how we can know that Jesus really did historically rise from the dead. There is also a chapter on why we can trust the Bible.

In this global environment, with so many belief systems competing for our attention, it is extremely important to understand the fundamentals of the Christian faith. This book was written to help you understand that faith in Jesus Christ is both valid and reasonable. It was also written to help you teach others why Christianity is true and why Jesus really is "the way, and the truth, and the life" (John 14:6a NASB).

Chapter 1

Does Truth Exist?

The Case for Absolute Truth

"What is truth?" retorted Pilate. With this he went out again to the Jews gathered there and said, "I find no basis for a charge against him." — John 18:38

"Sanctify them by the truth; your word is truth." — John 17:17

Jesus answered, "I am the way and the truth and the life. No one comes to the Father except through me." — John 14:6

Does truth really exist? Increasingly, skeptics argue there are no longer issues that are right or wrong for all people in all places. According to this postmodern worldview it is possible for something to be "true for you, but not true for me." In this nebulous world of skepticism and relativism, can a case still be made for absolute truth?

The case for truth begins with answering the question asked by Pilate to Jesus in John 18:38: "What is truth?" Pilate understood there were different sides to a story. The Jews wanted Jesus crucified, yet Pilate believed Jesus had done nothing worthy of death. Pilate vacillated between his belief in Jesus's innocence and his desire to please the crowd. His question about truth revealed the conflict that raged in his very soul. Pilate lived in a world where truth was determined by the emperor, who was believed to be the divine power of Rome. Power belonged to Rome because it wielded the sword and kept the masses in line through fear. Could it be that objective truth apart from the reality of Rome could exist?

Pilate's question echoes from the first century to contemporary society. People today struggle with the question of absolute truth. It is possible to deny the existence of absolutes, but does that mean absolute truth doesn't exist?

The first problem people who deny absolute truth must overcome is the claim there is no absolute truth. Those who defend this statement must overcome two concerns. First, if this statement includes itself, then the one making the statement would be guilty of what is known as "begging the question" or "circular reasoning," which means the validity of the statement lies within itself. If this statement is excluded, then the person is claiming an absolute while denying absolutes exist. In either case, how do you deny absolutes exist while making an absolute statement?

In his book, *I Don't Have Enough Faith to Be an Atheist*, Christian apologist Frank Turek offers a simple technique for pointing out circular reasoning. He calls it "the Road Runner Tactic."

> It reminds us of the cartoon characters Road Runner and Wile E. Coyote. As you may remember from Saturday morning cartoons, the Coyote's one and only quest is to chase down the speedy Road Runner and make him his evening meal. But the Road Runner is simply too fast and too smart. Just when the Coyote is gaining ground, the Road Runner stops short at the cliff's edge leaving the passing Coyote momentarily suspended in midair,

supported by nothing. As soon as the Coyote realizes he has no ground to stand on, he plummets to the valley floor and crashes in a heap.[1]

Using this tactic can help relativists come to the realization that their arguments collapse under the weight of their own illogical baggage. For example, if someone says to you, "All truth is relative, and there is no absolute truth," try taking the person's watch and seeing how he or she reacts. Of course, the person is going to say something like, "Hey, that's my watch and I want it back." All you have to say is, "Look, I'm just playing by your rules. Your truth says this watch belongs to you, but my truth says it belongs to me. Since all truth is relative, I have just as much claim to my truth as you do." At this point it is likely the police will be called to sort out what is true, and the person who really owns the watch is going to rely on an independent determination of truth based on reality in order to get the watch back.

A simple definition of truth is that which corresponds or operates within the boundaries of fact and corresponds with reality. This definition is known as the *correspondence theory of truth*. That is to say, truth is what is left when everything that is not true has been exposed and stripped away. There are two ways that something can be true: it can be *subjectively* true or it can be *objectively* true. For example, when I say, "Butterfinger candy bars are the best candy bars in the world," I have communicated something that is subjectively true because I have said something that corresponds to the reality of my opinion. It is true for *me* because it is *my* opinion. It is not necessarily true for the object in question (Butterfinger candy bars) because I am not offering independent facts that back up my assessment. But it is a true assessment of my opinion.

The second way something can be true is it can be objectively true. If I say, "Two plus two equals four," I am communicating a belief that I hold about an external, objective truth. Mathematical equations have one correct answer and may be proved to be either true or false. My individual taste has no bearing on the accuracy of the equation. As we consider truth claims, it is important to keep in mind the distinction between these two ways something can be true.

A second principle of truth is found in the *law of non-contradiction*. This law states that two opposing ideas cannot be both true and false at the same time. In other words, two plus two cannot equal four and two plus two equal five at the same time, under the same conditions. If two plus two equals four, then logically it cannot also equal five.

Skeptics who profess an Eastern worldview claim there is no absolute truth because everything is an illusion. However, this claim contradicts the reality that all people experience. You cannot say everything is an illusion unless there is some other clear reality to which it can be compared. Who is to say that this is not reality and something else is illusion or vice versa? Again, claiming the world is an illusion simply avoids reality; it does not provide an answer for our true existence.

In this chapter we will discuss four ways we can know truth: creation, conscience, Christ, and Scripture. Of course, God is not limited to these four ways, because we know He has spoken in other ways. In the Old Testament God spoke to His prophets and to others through dreams or visions. But the four areas we will discuss are ways we can understand truth today in order to grow in our walk with God and share Him with others.

Case #1: Creation

Genesis 1:1 begins with these familiar words: "In the beginning God created the heavens and the earth." God is the Supreme Being and Intelligent Designer who has made all things. As Paul said, "For by Him all things were created, both in the heavens and on earth, visible and invisible, whether thrones or dominions or rulers or authorities—all things have been created through Him and for Him" (Colossians 1:16 NASB).

How can God's creation reveal absolute truth? Psalm 19 explains:

> The heavens declare the glory of God;
> And the firmament shows His handiwork.
> Day unto day utters speech,
> And night unto night reveals knowledge.
> There is no speech nor language
> Where their voice is not heard.
> Their line has gone out through all the earth,
> And their words to the end of the world.
>
> In them He has set a tabernacle for the sun,
> Which is like a bridegroom coming out of his
>   chamber,
> And rejoices like a strong man to run its race.
> Its rising is from one end of heaven,
> And its circuit to the other end;

And there is nothing hidden from its heat.
(verses 1–6 NKJV)

Each aspect of creation reveals truth about the Creator. It proclaims God's glory, wisdom, power, and His care for all He has made.

As we consider the fact of creation, we see how another theory of truth is substantiated by the evidence that backs up a biblical understanding of the creation event. The *coherence theory* says that a given statement is true if it coheres with or does not contradict any other statements within a set of statements that also cohere with each other. A simpler way of saying this is that truth is internally consistent and never self-contradictory.

So let's look very briefly at the two main theories that explain how the universe came into existence. The world's best explanation is *Darwinian evolution*. In this theory the universe, or cosmos, as described by noted astronomer and astrophysicist Carl Sagan, "is all that is or ever was or ever will be."[2] In other words, the universe is eternal, and everything we see in it—the wonder of planetary orbits, the amazing cohesion demonstrated by how a myriad of laws and systems hold all things together, and the incomprehensible level of complexity we see when we look at this wondrous world—are all the product of a combination of blind chance and billions of years. Somehow the world formed itself from random cosmic matter, and primordial life emerged from the cosmic soup, eventually evolving from simple, single-celled creatures to the complex and highly evolved creatures of today. So that leaves us with an equation that says time plus chance plus natural law equals complexity on display at multiple levels of life.

The second theory of how all things came into being is found in Genesis 1:1: *"In the beginning God created the heavens and the earth."* It is as beautiful in its simplicity as it is powerful in its application. The universe is not eternal! It was called into existence by the voice of a holy God whose glory, wisdom, and power, as we saw in Psalm 19, are all on display. Evolutionists have been trying for decades to prove that the universe is eternal because the prevailing big bang theory presents them with an irrevocable truth. If the universe had a beginning, something outside of and beyond the scope of the universe must have caused it to happen. Spontaneous generation (life coming from nonlife) is a scientific impossibility, but most evolutionists would rather embrace the absurd than bow to the existence of absolute truth rooted in an eternal God.

The fossil record should be filled with hundreds of thousands of examples of intermediary life forms that are gradually transitioning from the simple to the complex. But even Darwin admitted the fossil record is unexplainably incomplete. Concerning the record Darwin said, "The number of intermediate varieties, which have formerly existed, [must] be truly enormous. Why then is not every geological formation and every stratum full of such intermediate links? Geology assuredly does not reveal any such finely-graded organic chain; and this, perhaps, is the most obvious and serious objection which can be urged against the theory."[3]

The fossil record that exists today is less complete than the record of Darwin's day. However, scientists continue to insist evolution is the only plausible theory of origins, because if you reject evolution you are left with having to admit there is a God who created the universe.

One more coherent line of thinking should be considered as we look at creation as an example of truth. In 1996 microbiologist Michael Behe rocked the evolutionary world with his book *Darwin's Black Box: The Biochemical Challenge to Evolution.* Dr. Behe (who was raised Catholic but does not consider himself to be a believer) points out that Darwin, using the technology available in the nineteenth century, would have seen the human cell as nothing more than a black blob. He couldn't have possibly known that inside that black blob was a microworld of incredible complexity on multiple levels. Cells are not simple structures but rather complex machines that indicate they are much too complex to have evolved by random chance. Speaking of Darwin's limited understanding of biology, Behe said, "In Darwin's day, the cell was thought to be so simple that first-rate scientists such as Thomas Huxley and Ernst Haeckel could seriously think that it might arise spontaneously from sea mud, which would be quite congenial to Darwinism. Even just fifty years ago it was a lot easier to believe that Darwinian evolution might explain the foundation of life."[4]

Dr. Behe coined the term *irreducible complexity* to describe systems that are so complex that they cannot be the result of slight, successive modifications of a preclusive system, because if any one part of the system is missing it cannot function. To illustrate this principle, Behe holds up a common, simple mousetrap that has five working parts. Using the evolutionary model all five parts would have to appear at the same time and be fully functional for the trap to work. He points out that if any of the five working parts cease to function the trap is useless.

Think about it this way . . . scientists have estimated that it would take at least fifty thousand separate changes for a water based organism to transition to a land based organism. With that in mind, let's simplify it even further by imagining a typical fish. If a fish evolves legs without lungs it will walk out of the ocean and suffocate. If it gets lungs without legs it will drown. Just like the mouse trap illustration, an organism transitioning from water to land would have to develop all of the land based necessities for life at the same time to survive.

In addition, creation is a universal way in which God has revealed Himself to humanity. The book of Romans teaches, "For since the creation of the world His invisible attributes, His eternal power and divine nature, have been clearly seen, being understood through what has been made, so that they are without excuse"(1:20 NASB). Creation is one clear way every person in the world knows God exists. Since the advent of the electron microscope, human beings can now look with awe into the black box and comprehend in a limited and finite way the formerly "invisible attributes, His eternal power and divine nature." Before microbiology we could see and comprehend only the result of God's invisible attributes. Now we can see and partially understand not only *what* God has done but also the *how*.

Case #2: Conscience

God has given every person a sense of right and wrong. There is an undeniable moral sense found within each human being. While two people may have different standards of right and wrong, every person believes certain things are right and other things are evil. Paul said, "For when Gentiles who do not have the Law do instinctively the things of the Law, these, not having the Law, are a law to themselves, in that they show the work of the Law written in their hearts, their conscience bearing witness and their thoughts alternately accusing or else defending them" (Romans 2:14–15 NASB).

This includes the sin nature that lives within every person. Romans 3:23 teaches, "All have sinned and fall short of the glory of God." We know we are imperfect, and apart from Christ, we also feel the need for forgiveness. The very fact that we know we need forgiveness indicates that we, likewise, realize we have committed some wrong. This wrong is considered wrong because of our conscience and implies that we have transgressed against an absolute moral standard.

There are some who argue that universal moral law doesn't exist. They say that what Christians call moral law is actually nothing more than instincts that have developed as part of the evolutionary concept of self-preservation. We act in certain ways that we describe as moral because evolution has taught us that those certain ways lead to survival. Others say moral laws are culturally developed since morality varies from culture to culture.

So let's look at the logic of these arguments. I submit that there is no one who really believes all morality is relative. If you encounter such a person, simply take something that belongs to him and he will cry foul. He will immediately say something like, "That's not fair," or "How would you like it if I did that to you?" The moment that happens he has to admit he has walked into a self-defeating argument. If there is no moral law that transcends personal opinion, then what is the "that" he is referring to when he says, "That's not fair." If his opinion says something isn't fair, then who is to say his opinion about what is fair should be superior? You might ask that person, "Excuse me, did you write the book on fairness?" If the answer is no, then to what standard is he referring? True moral disagreements are not possible unless there is an absolute moral standard that transcends personal opinion. If all opinions and standards are equally valid, we have no grounds to condemn or hold accountable the perpetrators of the Nazi holocaust.

What about the idea that morality is simply a by-product of survival of the fittest? This argument breaks down, because it cannot explain the existence of altruistic behavior. Suppose you are walking past a farm pond, and you see someone in the pond who is obviously drowning. You know you are not a strong swimmer, but you feel compelled to try to save this person's life even at the risk of your own. Evolution could never be responsible for the idea of self-sacrifice. That would run counter to the evolutionary idea of personal survival above all else. When the World Trade Center was attacked on September 11, 2001, the natural impulse, the evolutionary impulse, would have been to flee for your life. And yet we know there were police officers and firefighters who ran into the buildings and demonstrated total disregard for personal safety.

Finally, what about the idea that morality is culturally developed? First, as far as we know, there are no cultures that reward and glorify cowardice. There are no cultures where people have developed the idea that murder is something to be cherished. No matter how primitive or sophisticated, cultures around the world share a disdain for cowards and murderers.

Some would point to India and say, "Wait a minute . . . in India people believe cows are sacred and must be protected, but in the West we raise cows for food. Doesn't that prove diversity in cultural value systems?" It might, until you ask why cows are considered sacred in India. Hinduism embraces reincarnation, the idea that the souls of departed loved ones return in lower life forms. Since many Hindus in India believe eating cows would be equivalent to consuming a person, they forbid eating them. Since people in the West are also appalled by the idea of cannibalism, it turns out our cultural values are in line.

Case #3: Scripture teaches truth is a person . . . Jesus Christ

Truth is something that most people seek; no one enjoys sifting through lies, hypocrisy, or deceit. Just as a businessman wants to know the truth about the person he is conducting business with, people want to know the truth about God. The good news is, God has made truth accessible to all people through Jesus Christ. Truth is not some abstract idea that is impossible to attain as contemporary society would suggest, but rather truth is a person—the person Jesus Christ. Jesus said, "I am the way, the truth, and the life. No one comes to the Father except through Me" (John 14:6 NKJV). He is the absolute and final truth. People need not search for truth in any other person or concept. God has given us His truth through the Lord Jesus Christ! This statement by Jesus sets Christianity apart from every other religious system or thought process in the world. Jesus is uniquely and specifically the truth. Accepting Christ means accepting the truth.

But these words Jesus spoke are contained within the pages of the Christian Bible. Two things have to be demonstrably true in order for us to rationally believe that Jesus Christ is the truth. First, the Scripture that contains this saying of Jesus must be reliable. Second, Jesus had to be right about His own identity. It could be possible for the scriptural account of Jesus saying He is the truth to be true but that Jesus was just a prophet who was wrong about His own identity.

Let's briefly break it down. Is the Bible true? Can it be trusted? You could fill a library with the books that have been written to answer that question, but let's consider just a few facts. Literary scholars agree the more manuscripts (copies of a document) you have, the more likely it is you can rely on their accuracy. The New Testament, which contains the statement Jesus made about truth, certainly passes the manuscript test. There are at least 5,700 copies of the New Testament in Greek. When you add the 19,000 copies written in other languages, there is a minimum of 25,000 copies of the New Testament. And thanks to modern archaeological methods, that number is rising every year as more and more manuscripts are discovered. The closest document from antiquity we have in number of copies is Homer's *Iliad* with

643 manuscripts known to exist. And yet no serious scholar questions the accuracy or authorship of the *Iliad*.

So there are a lot of copies of the New Testament. How do we know those copies are accurate? Textual scholars want not only a large number of copies, they want copies that can be traced back as close as possible to the original document. The earliest undisputed manuscript we have of the New Testament is a portion of the Gospel of John that dates back as far as AD 117. Most of the New Testament can be found in something called the Chester Beatty Papyri, which dates back to AD 250. Compare this to the biography of Alexander the Great, which has a four hundred-year gap between the events of Alexander's life and the emergence of his biography. And yet, just as no one questions the *Iliad*, no one questions the fact that Alexander the Great actually lived.

Two other points on the reliability of Scripture should be made. First, we know that at least three of the four Gospels were all written before AD 60. The Gospels are eyewitness accounts of the life of Jesus (including His death and resurrection). Since Jesus died in AD 33, we know that there were many eyewitnesses still alive at the time three of the Gospels (Matthew, Mark, and Luke, or the Synoptic Gospels) were written. The fact that we have three eyewitness accounts of Jesus's life written so close to the actual events, and to have those accounts line up almost perfectly, provides near indisputable evidence that the Bible is accurate and can be trusted.

Second, archaeological discoveries verify the truthfulness of the Gospel accounts. Skeptics have long said that the science of archaeology will one day contradict the Bible. Well, the science of archaeology has been around a long time, and not one discovery contradicts the Scripture. In fact, every significant archaeological discovery has supported, not contradicted, the Scripture. For years skeptics said King David was a mythical, composite Israelite king who never actually existed. Then an upright stone called a stele, which was used as a monument to memorialize an important event, was discovered with the carved inscription, "House of David." This stele affirms the existence of a united monarchy under King David.

As we said, the fact Scripture is true doesn't necessarily mean Jesus was right about being the way, the truth, and the life. So how can we know that what Jesus said about Himself is true? Jesus's statements about Himself all hinge on the veracity of the resurrection. It would be reasonable to believe that if Jesus really did rise from the dead three days after His crucifixion, then He is God in the flesh, and His understanding of Himself is true. What about the evidence for the crucifixion? There are many verifiers, but let's boil the list down to four:

- Jesus's death by crucifixion;
- the disciples belief in the appearances of Jesus;
- the empty tomb;
- the conversion of the church persecutor, Paul, and the skeptic James.

Jesus's death by crucifixion is, in the words of Jesus Seminar skeptic John Dominic Crossan, "as sure as anything historical can ever be."⁵ It is confirmed by Matthew, Mark, Luke, and John in the four Gospels that bear their names. It is also confirmed by a number of non-Christian sources, including Josephus, Tacitus, Lucian of Samosata, Suetonius, Thallus, and the Jewish Talmud. The fact of Jesus's crucifixion is as certain as any historical event can be. The fact He actually died on the cross, not fainted and was later revived by the coolness of the tomb, is proved by common sense. Crucifixion was a brutal, violent, merciless form of human torture and death. Jesus was scourged within an inch of His life before being nailed to the cross. In addition to the blood loss from the scourging and the wounds to His hands and feet, His side was pierced to make sure He was dead. It is not reasonable to believe that a man who suffered this much torture somehow survived the wounds and still had the strength to push back the stone, walk out of the tomb, and convince His disciples that He had risen from the dead.

There can be no doubt Jesus's disciples believed He rose from the dead. We have the eyewitness accounts of the empty tomb in the Gospels; the attempt by the Jewish leaders to spread a false story explaining why the tomb was empty; the eyewitness accounts of the appearance of the resurrected Christ to the disciples on three occasions; plus a number of other witnesses (Paul says more than five hundred in 1 Corinthians 15:6); and the fact that eleven of the twelve disciples died painful deaths rather than recant their testimony of seeing the risen Christ. While it is true someone might in reality die for a lie that he believes to be the truth, it is also true that a person does not die for something he knows to be false.

Also, the disciples' lives were dramatically changed by their belief in the risen Christ. Peter went from a rash, irresponsible, and cowardly fisherman to being the dynamic leader of the church in Jerusalem. James was transformed from skeptic to martyr, and Paul went from being a stone-cold persecutor of the church to being its greatest missionary.

If the Scripture is reliable, and all the evidence says that it is; and if it testifies to the fact that Jesus said He is the truth; and if Jesus really was crucified and then raised from the dead; it proves what He said about Himself is true, and He is the living embodiment of truth.

Life Answers

In this chapter, we have made the case for the existence of absolute truth. Belief in absolute truth is essential for the Christian, because it is what keeps us tethered to reality, and it forms the foundation of our confidence in the voracity of God's Word. While absolute truth cannot be demonstrated, it can be believed beyond a reasonable doubt, and it can be demonstrated through life experiences. We experience absolute truth every time we encounter facts that align perfectly with reality. Anything that falls outside that alignment is false, and since everything that doesn't correspond to the facts of an established reality is disqualified by failing to reflect the corresponding reality, what is left must be the absolute truth.

We have established the existence of absolute truth using the coherence theory, which is demonstrated in the glory of creation through the miracle of microbiology and through the facts of the fossil record. We have demonstrated the existence of absolute truth in a universal moral law that guides our thinking and transcends purely cultural influences. Finally, we have demonstrated the existence of absolute truth by pointing to the truth claims of Jesus Christ. Those claims are verified by the evidence presented in the four Gospels, which were written during the lifetime of the eyewitnesses, verified by all available archaeological evidence, and demonstrated to be true by the fact of the resurrection and the reaction of Jesus's disciples.

Remember, when all the arguments have been presented, considered, and either accepted or rejected, truth is ultimately found in the person of Jesus Christ. This truth makes Jesus the only way to get to the Father and, therefore, the only way we can know we have eternal life.

Points to Remember

1. Persons who claim absolutes do not exist cannot reasonably make that argument, because their claim is an absolute in itself.

2. God's creation reveals truth by proclaiming His glory, wisdom, power, and care for all He has made (Psalm 19:1–6).

3. Man's conscience reveals truth. While two people may have different standards of right and wrong, every person believes certain things are right and other things are evil (Romans 2:14–15).

4. Truth is found in Jesus Christ, who is "the way and the truth and the life" (John 14:6).

Notes

[1] Frank Turek, *I Don't Have Enough Faith to Be an Atheist* (Wheaton, IL: Crossway, 2004), 39.

[2] Carl Sagan, *Cosmos* (New York: Ballentine Books, 1985), 1.

[3] Charles Darwin, *The Origin of Species* (New York: P. F. Collies and Son, 1902), 55.

[4] Behe, Michael J., *Darwin's Black Box: The Biochemical Challenge to Evolution* (New York: Free Press, 2006), 271.

[5] John Dominic Crossan, *Jesus: A Revolutionary Biography* (San Francisco: HarperCollins, 1991), 145.

Chapter 2

Does God Exist?

Four Reasons We Can Know God Is Real

Yet for us there is but one God, the Father, from whom all things came and for whom we live; and there is but one Lord, Jesus Christ, through whom all things came and through whom we live. — 1 Corinthians 8:6

And without faith it is impossible to please God, because anyone who comes to him must believe that he exists and that he rewards those who earnestly seek him. — Hebrews 11:6

The modern world is filled with skepticism, especially regarding Christianity. Frequently, Christianity is represented negatively in the news, and people often attempt to disprove it by simply removing God, the heart of the faith. If God does not exist, then Christianity must be a false religion, and Christians have no basis upon which to stake their entire system of belief. Because so many people are attempting to prove that God does not exist, it follows that it is important for Christians to learn how to provide reason and evidence that God *does* exist. Historically, there are four main arguments that Christians have used to explain His existence: the cosmological argument, the teleological argument, the moral argument, and the experiential argument. Before you become overwhelmed, remember that these are just scientific words to explain simple arguments about creation's existence, creation's design, human morality, and personal experience, respectively. By knowing these four arguments, you will be well prepared to defend the existence of God.

Cosmological Argument

The cosmological argument states that because the universe has a cause, only a creator could have made it; otherwise the universe would just simply exist without purpose or cause. There are many popular theories regarding the cosmological argument, but perhaps one of the more famous is called the Leibnizian Cosmological Argument. The argument is as follows:

1. Anything that exists has an explanation of its existence.
2. If the universe has an explanation of its existence, that explanation is God.
3. The universe exists.
4. Therefore, the universe has an explanation of its existence.
5. Therefore, the explanation of the existence of the universe is God.[1]

Now that you have read the argument, take a deep breath, and let's go through this slowly.

First, Leibniz suggested that anything in existence must have an explanation of how it exists. Take yourself, for example. Can you explain how you were created? Or what about the building you are inside right now? Can you explain how it was created? Of course you can. We know it takes procreation to create a new human and that it takes a builder to build a building. You and the building have an explanation of your existence. This is all the first point is essentially stating.

Second, if the universe exists, the only explanation can be God. Now this may seem a little narrow-minded to nonbelievers, but ask them how they believe the universe was created. Many will say the big bang or another theory that science has provided to explain the creation of the universe. The only problem is, science can only explain how creation happened, it cannot explain the beginning of creation. For example, the big bang can explain that there was a point of infinite temperature and density holding the matter that formed the universe from which the bang occurred, but this theory cannot explain where that matter came from. Think of it this way: many naturalist views of creation can explain how a house is built, but they cannot explain where all the block, wood, and other building materials came from. In the case of the universe, the building material of the universe cannot be explained apart from God. Thus, if the universe has an explanation of its existence, it *must* be God.

The argument concludes by acknowledging that the universe exists. Because it exists, it must have an explanation of its existence, and that explanation can only be God. In a simpler way, this argument states that anything that exists has an explanation of its existence; and in the case of the universe, any explanation apart from God fails to adequately explain every aspect of creation.

Many scientists argue that the universe is eternal . . . that it has always existed. The problem with this argument is that all the scientific evidence suggests this is just not true. Without getting into the weeds of complicated scientific theory that involve the makeup of the universe, the fact that the universe is expanding (not just the content of the universe expanding into empty space but space itself is expanding); the discovery of the existence of residual radiation generated by the heat of the initial creation; and slight variations in the temperature of cosmic background radiation all point to a universe that wasn't and then—quite suddenly—was.

Another important aspect of the cosmological argument is that it provides purpose to creation. If the universe and all that is in it is the result of a colossal accident, then the universe and all life that is found in the universe is meaningless. The very fact that we would ask questions about meaning and purpose in life suggests that we innately sense there *is* meaning and purpose. When we build something with our hands out of wood or some other material we begin with a plan that suggests a purpose. When we are finished building we look at what we have built and ask ourselves if the finished product fulfills the purpose of that plan. Isaiah reminds us that God created the earth for the purpose of being home to beings He ultimately fashioned in His own image. Isaiah said, "For thus says the LORD, who created the heavens (He is the God who formed the earth and made it, He established it and did not create it a waste place, but formed it to be inhabited)" (Isaiah 45:18 NASB). So God created the heavens (the universe) for the purpose of containing the earth that would be suitable for, and inhabited by, humans created in His image.

Everyone at some point in life asks the question, "What is the meaning of life?" We have all seen portrayed in movies, commercials, and TV shows the man who climbs to the top of some high mountain to pose that question to a lone guru. This knowledge that we naturally long for was placed in us by our Creator so that we would search for Him. One of the early church fathers, Augustine of Hippo, said, "Thou hast made us for thyself, and restless is our heart until it comes to rest in thee."[2]

The book of Genesis says:

> Then God said, "Let Us make man in Our image, according to Our likeness; and let them rule over the fish of the sea and over the birds of the sky and over the cattle and over all the earth, and over every creeping thing that creeps on the earth." God created man in His own image, in the image of God He created him; male and female He created them. God blessed them; and God said to them, "Be fruitful and multiply, and fill the earth, and subdue it; and rule over the fish of the sea and over the birds of the sky and over every living thing that moves on the earth." (1:26–28 NASB)

The purpose statement for the creation of men and women finds its home in the creation purpose of God. God is a relational being, and because He is relational He created us for three reasons:

1. to have a personal relationship with the Creator;

2. to have relationships with each other;

3. to work within those relationships to care for the created order.

Having a personal relationship with God gives us meaning and purpose in life. Because we are finite creatures, our lives would lack any meaning past the duration of our own physical existence if we were not in a relationship with God. A prominent talk show host once stated that he "sometimes felt as though his heart had a hole in it through which a cold wind blew."[3] Solomon echoed the same sentiment in Ecclesiastes 2:11,

> Yet when I surveyed all that my hands had done
>   and what I had toiled to achieve,
> everything was meaningless, a chasing after the
>   wind;
>   nothing was gained under the sun.

Solomon was the wisest and wealthiest man who ever lived. He did not deny himself any desire or pleasure, and yet when he looked at his reflection, he saw the certainty of his own death and the meaninglessness of his life apart from God. Solomon recognized that the solution to his feeling that all is vanity was, "Remember also your Creator in the days of your youth, before the evil days come and the years draw near when you will say, 'I have no delight in them'" (Ecclesiastes 12:1 NASB).

Next, God created both male and female as more than just a social convenience. He created them to complement and fulfill each other and to fulfill His divine plan to fill the earth with relational beings who would ultimately need a Savior to redeem them from their sin. The ultimate purpose of humanity is to glorify God and love Him forever. Part of that purpose is fulfilled in the glorification of God's Son when He died on the cross to atone for our sin. His resurrection from the dead glorified His Father and established Him as both Redeemer and Ruler of the created order. When we receive Christ as our Savior it is to the glory of God and through the glory of His Son, Jesus.

Finally, God pronounced His creation "very good," and He set humanity as the stewards of all He had made (Genesis 1:28, 31). We are called to work in fellowship with Him to care for and rule over His creation. We care for the environment, and we enter into the creative process when we learn, create, and explore.

Here are the most important aspects to remember about this argument:

1. The universe must have an explanation for its existence; therefore, God is the only explanation that succeeds in explaining every aspect of the universe's existence.

2. Only a created universe can have purpose. We know from God's Word that He created the world to be inhabited and that the beings He created to inhabit the earth were made for a relationship with Him, for each other, and for the purpose of glorying Him by entering into His creative work and being caretakers of His creation.

The Teleological Argument

The teleological argument is an academic term that means simply that the universe is so well designed and finely tuned, it could only be the product of a creator. Though many Darwinists and naturalists have asserted that the universe exists through a series of evolutionary processes, this theory fails to take into account the complexity of the design of the universe. The apparent design of the universe can only be attributed to a designer.

One of the most famous examples of this argument is from William Paley's "Watchmaker" parable.

In crossing a heath, suppose I pitched my foot against a *stone*, and were asked how the stone came to be there, I might possibly answer, that, for any thing I knew to the contrary, it had lain there for ever: nor would it perhaps be very easy to show the absurdity of this answer. But suppose I had found a *watch* upon the ground, and it should be enquired how the watch happened to be in that place; I should hardly think of the answer which I had before given, that, for any thing I knew, the watch might have always been there. Yet why should not this answer serve for the watch, as well as for the stone? Why is it not as admissible in the second case, as in the first? For this reason, and for no other, viz. that, when we come to inspect the watch, we perceive (what we could not discover in the stone) that its several parts are framed and put together for a purpose, e. g. that they are so formed and adjusted as to produce motion, and that motion so regulated as to point out the hour of the day; that, if the several parts had been differently shaped from what they are, of a different size from what they are, or placed after any other manner, or in any other order, than that in which they are placed, either no motion at all would have been carried on in the machine, or none which would have answered the use that is now served by it. . . . This mechanism being observed (it requires indeed an examination of the instrument, and perhaps some previous knowledge of the subject, to perceive and understand it; but being once, as we have said, observed and understood), the inference, we think, is inevitable; that the watch must have had a maker, that there must have existed, at some time and at some place or other, an artificer or artificers who formed it for the purpose which we find it actually to answer; who comprehended its construction, and designed its use.[4]

According to Paley, the watch demands a different verdict than the rock simply because its design proves that it had a creator. Similarly, the universe is so finely tuned and designed that it demands a creator for its existence. A more modern example of this argument comes from Michael Behe, in a concept called *irreducible complexity.*

Irreducible complexity is the idea that many molecular machines are simply too complex to have formed by evolution. Behe demonstrates this idea using bacterial flagellum. He contends that the flagellum, which moves by propelling itself using a paddling mechanism, "is necessarily composed of at least three parts—a paddle, a rotor, and a motor—it is irreducibly complex."[5] Behe's argument is that because of the complexity of this organism, evolution cannot explain its origin, because if one member of this system is absent it cannot work. Thus, evolution's contention that the flagellum evolved into this system from a Darwinian selection mechanism through bacteria without a flagellum cannot stand to reason.[6]

In addition to these arguments, consider the following statistics that show just how finely tuned the universe is:

- The electromagnetic coupling constant binds electrons to protons in atoms. If it was smaller, fewer electrons could be held. If it was larger, electrons would be held too tightly to bond with other atoms.

- Ratio of electron to proton mass (1:1836). Again, if this was larger or smaller, molecules could not form.

- Carbon and oxygen nuclei have finely tuned energy levels.

- Electromagnetic and gravitational forces are finely tuned, so the right kind of star can be stable.

- Our sun is the right [color]. If it was redder or bluer, photosynthetic response would be weaker.

- Our sun is also the right mass. If it was larger, its brightness would change too quickly and there would be too much high energy radiation. If it was smaller, the range of planetary distances able to support life would be too narrow; the right distance would be so close to the star that tidal forces would disrupt the planet's rotational period. UV radiation would also be inadequate for photosynthesis.

- The earth's distance from the sun is crucial for a stable water cycle. Too far away, and most water would freeze; too close and most water would boil.

- The earth's gravity, axial tilt, rotation period, magnetic field, crust thickness, oxygen/nitrogen ratio, carbon dioxide, water [vapor] and ozone levels are just right.[7]

Obviously, the universe is a product of design and of fine-tuning, and only a creator could do that!

Moral Argument

The moral argument for the existence of God is very simple. This argument suggests that without God there can be no foundation for morality. If God is our Creator, then we are accountable to Him. Yet, if God is not our Creator, we are accountable to no one. If we are accountable to God as Creator, His standard of morality becomes an objective morality. Yet, if we are accountable to no one, then morality is subjective and what may be moral for me is not moral for you. Each person chooses his or her own morality. Therefore, if objective morals exist, God must exist too. Here is another way of stating the argument:

1. If God does not exist, objective morals do not either.

2. Objective morals do exist.

3. Therefore, God exists.

However, though some opinions on moral issues may differ from person to person, such as cursing, drinking, and so forth, there are many acts that are considered universally immoral. For example, there are laws against murder, rape, and theft in just about every culture in the world. These three acts are therefore objective morals, because the collective world is in agreement that they are immoral and wrong, and just because someone does not believe these three things to be wrong does not exempt the person from justice and punishment for these heinous crimes.

Examples can be found in Hollywood portrayals as well. We have all seen movies or TV shows that place the main character(s) in an integrity predicament. Perhaps the main character must choose to lie and keep his job or tell the truth and lose it. Maybe she must choose to cheat on her husband or remain faithful to her spouse. Maybe the main character must choose to remain poor by refusing to take part in a shady business deal—or maybe the character chooses to take part in the deal and ruin comes to him or her later. Ultimately, all of these situations convey one message: there is a universal morality that many people consider right or wrong, or good or bad. The moral argument simply declares that this universal morality exists only because we have the same Creator who has one set of morals that has been instilled inside His creation.

Experiential Argument

Perhaps the experiential argument is the easiest to understand because it comes from personal experience. Have you had an encounter with God? If so, this encounter comes as proof of God's existence. The Bible teaches in 2 Corinthians 5:17 that Christians are a new creation after giving their life to Christ. In this sense, this life changing encounter is a testament to God's existence. Think about the story of Paul in the Bible. Before Paul was a Christian, he did not believe that Jesus Christ was the Messiah and he persecuted Christians. Yet, when he experienced Christ on the road to Damascus, he was changed, and he shared that experience with King Agrippa in Acts 26 in an attempt to persuade Agrippa of Christ's existence.

Whatever your experience, you can use that to teach people about God. Tell them about how He has given you peace in times of turmoil. Tell them about your salvation experience. Tell them how God has provided for you in times when you were struggling financially. Tell them how He has answered your prayers time and time again. All of these stories are valid reasons to believe in God. Perhaps your own experiences will lead someone to experience Him!

Life Answers

We have presented the four reasons that God exists: the cosmological argument, the teleological argument, the moral argument, and the experiential argument. Now that you have studied these four arguments, plan to use them this week to help others who doubt the existence of God learn that there are substantial reasons to believe He indeed does exist!

Points to Remember

1. Only God can provide an adequate explanation to the creation and purpose of the universe.

2. The design and fine-tuning of the universe is so precise that an accident of nature could never explain its creation; only God as Creator can.

3. The objective morals that exist innately around the world suggest that one creator made all humans.

4. Your experiences with God can prove that God is real to others.

Notes

[1] William Lane Craig, "The Existence of God (1)," *Reasonable Faith* (Wheaton, IL: Crossway, 2008), 106.

[2] *The Confessions of St. Augustine*, trans. and ed. Albert Cook Outler (Mineola, NY: Dover Publications), 1.

[3] Ken Hemphill, *Life Answers: Making Sense of Your World* (Nashville: Life-Way Press), 84.

[4] William Paley, "State of the Argument," *Natural Theology* (New York: Oxford University Press, 2006), 7–8.

[5] Michael J. Behe, *Darwin's Black Box: The Biochemical Challenge to Evolution* (New York: Free Press, 2006), 72.

[6] William A. Dembski, "The Emergence of Irreducibly Complex Systems," *No Free Lunch* (Oxford: Rowman & Littlefield, 2002), 251.

[7] Quoted from "The Universe is Finely Tuned for Life," Answers in Genesis, May 10, 1997, last modified 2015, https://answersingenesis.org /evidence-for-creation/the-universe-is-finely-tuned-for-life/.

Chapter 3

Are Miracles Possible?

The Evidence to Support the Existence of Miracles

"He performs wonders that cannot be fathomed,
miracles that cannot be counted." — Job 5:9

Miracles are an interesting part of the Bible, and they play a specific role in encouraging our faith. Though the discussion of miracles often focuses solely on those Jesus performed, miracles are found throughout the Bible. From Genesis to Revelation, miracles are interwoven throughout Scripture and are essential to many of the most popular stories of the Bible. Consider the miracle of the parting of the Red Sea. What about the defeat by Gideon of the numberless Midianite army? God used three hundred Israelites (after sending 31,700 home!) to win a great battle, therefore putting His great miracle-working power on display. Then, of course, there is the fact that God raised Jesus from the dead, which is the greatest recorded miracle in the Bible. Unfortunately, however, miracles are not only the subject of stories in the Bible, they are also the subject of objections to the Bible. Many nonbelievers, and even some who claim to be believers, reject the idea that the miracles in the Bible actually happened.

Christians who reject biblical miracles will often tell you that the miracles are irrelevant to the story of the gospel and to the purpose of the Bible. They will claim that the miracles Jesus performed, such as turning water into wine, healing people, exorcising demons, or cursing a fig tree have no bearing on the gospel message. However, consider that the hope of Christianity lies in the miracle of the resurrection of Christ, who came to earth through the miracle of the virgin birth. Bearing that in mind, miracles are an essential part of the story of Christ and redemption. Ultimately, Christianity will stand or fall upon the existence of miracles, as our hope lies in the greatest miracle of all.

Objections to Miracles

Before explaining the evidence for miracles, it is important to understand the objections a Christian may face when speaking to someone about miracles.

Objection #1: Many people have never witnessed a genuine miracle. They have not seen a miraculous healing brought about through prayer and the laying on of hands. They have not seen someone raised from the dead. I doubt anyone would say he or she has seen an entire sea parted after someone stretched out a staff over the water. So, one of the most popular objections against the existence of miracles is that since they are very uncommon in modern society, they could not have occurred in the first-century world of Jesus.

Objection #2: Miracles violate the laws of nature. Since the acceptance of Newtonian physics, there has been a general understanding of the laws that govern nature. For example, when Isaac Newton saw an apple fall from a tree, he began to study why it fell. His conclusion is now known as the law of gravity—objects beyond a certain density will fall to the earth because the gravity is so strong. Anything that violates this law would be considered a miracle. If an apple fell up instead of down, it would violate the law of gravity. However, because Newton's theory is considered a natural law, people have accepted as fact that it cannot and will not be violated. Therefore, Jesus's ascension would be a violation of the law of gravity.

Objection #3: The recording of miracles only occurs in superstitious cultures or in cultures of barbaric people. In other words, civilized societies cannot believe in miracles because miraculous stories only originate from primitive societies or those societies that participate in superstitious practices.

Divine Origin of Miracles

One of the most important things to understand about miracles is they are of a divine origin. In other words, we cannot expect miracles to have a natural appearance, because the definition of a miracle suggests it is contradictory to natural law. Miracles in the Bible were for a divine purpose, and they were brought about by divine power. "So Jesus said to them, 'Truly, truly, I say to you, the Son can do nothing of his own accord, but only what he sees the Father doing. For whatever the Father does, that the Son does likewise'" (John 5:19 ESV). Jesus acknowledged that His power came from above. Therefore, the miracles Jesus did were not on His own, but they were performed through the power of the one who sent Him (verse 30). Even the resurrection was accomplished by the power of God. Acts 2:24 says, "But God raised him from the dead, freeing him from the agony of death, because it was impossible for death to keep its hold on him." This idea of divine origin is important because it traces all miracles back to God, the all-powerful Creator of the universe, and makes the idea of miracles a little easier to believe.

The character and existence of God also plays a role in the evidence for miracles. Consider what we learned in the last chapter while studying the reasons we can know God exists. If God exists, there is an immediate belief in the supernatural. Miracles immediately become more believable, since anyone who believes in God has accepted the idea of the supernatural. If God is supernatural, and the world in which we live is natural, then every time God reveals Himself we experience a miracle! When God spoke to Samuel, He spoke to him audibly. Speaking audibly is nothing unusual; however, the simple fact that it was God speaking to Samuel and not another human is miraculous because God is supernatural. Think about other instances recorded in Scripture that God revealed Himself to humans. In Exodus 3, God revealed Himself to Moses through a burning bush. Later in Exodus, God revealed Himself to Moses again by hiding Moses in the cleft of a rock and allowing him to see a small part of His glory. God revealed Himself to Jacob in a dream. In the New Testament, God revealed Himself to Paul in a bright light. He revealed Himself to both Ananias and Peter through visions. The fact that God is supernatural makes any action, appearance, or revelation of Himself in the natural world a miracle. In this sense, belief in a God who is active in the world and in the lives of believers can explain miracles.

The only objection that can be raised to this necessity of miracles is to assert that God is not active in the world or in believers' lives. However, the Bible depicts God as being very involved throughout history, from His creation of the world in Genesis 1, all the way to the end of the book of Revelation. God sometimes causes natural disasters such as the flood of Noah's time. He directs nations, as He did when He allowed Syria to take Israel captive and scatter them; also, later directing Babylon to take the kingdom of Judah captive. God caused the sun to stand still for Joshua and the skies to darken at the crucifixion of Jesus. Individually, God caused Pharaoh's heart to harden in Exodus and softened Paul's heart on the road to Damascus. The Bible is full of examples that demonstrate how God is active throughout the world at all times. Therefore, the objection that God is not active in the world and in the lives of individuals cannot stand against the revelation of the Bible.

A Different Understanding of the Natural

As stated earlier in the chapter, a common objection to miracles is that because miracles are acts that defy the laws of nature, they cannot exist, since the laws of nature cannot be broken. For example, the virgin birth could never have happened because Mary, according to the laws of nature, could never have received the Y chromosome needed to conceive the boy Jesus without a man. The first response to this is simply that God is God; He possesses all the attributes of divinity (omnipotence, omniscience, omnipresence) and can do whatever He desires. That may sound elementary and closed-minded, but if we believe God to be all-powerful, then it becomes easier to believe in the miracles God performs. William Lane Craig, a famous apologist, says that the virgin birth was one of the largest stumbling blocks to his coming to faith; but after believing that God created the world, he realized that a God powerful enough to create something from nothing would certainly be powerful enough to cause a virgin to conceive.[1] God created the world and sustains it, so it is logical and reasonable to believe that He can do what He chooses in the world, whether or not it is perceived as a miracle. As the psalmist said,

> Whatever the LORD pleases, he does,
>   in heaven and on earth,
>   in the seas and all deeps. (Psalm 135:6 ESV)

Another response to the objection of miracles, based on their violation of the laws of nature, is to realize we simply do not know with certainty God's definition of natural and supernatural. Humans assign those categories to God based on our limited understanding of Him and of the laws of nature. What finite creatures, who are limited by matter, time, and space, consider to be miracles may be natural occurrences to God, who knows no limits. We are learning new things about the cosmos every day. For example, prior to the Wright Brothers' successful flight in 1903, humans flying through the air by any means would have been considered a miracle. But the force of lift that allows a heavier than air machine to fly through the air is part of natural law, which was discovered and applied to the idea of human flight. What appeared to be a miracle or supernatural event to us is actually part of God's design of the universe. This is not to say that all miracles are undiscovered natural laws, because we know that many miracles are simply God's direct intervention. But a partial explanation of miracles might be that miracles from our perspective are simply normal operating procedure for God.

Miracles Defended by the Jews and Scripture

The Jewish people of Jesus's day did not dismiss His miracles or proclaim that He had no power. On the contrary, they believed the miracles because they were eyewitnesses. However, they misattributed the source of Jesus's power. "Then a demon-oppressed man who was blind and mute was brought to him, and he healed him, so that the man spoke and saw. And all the people were amazed, and said, 'Can this be the Son of David?' But when the Pharisees heard it, they said, 'It is only by Beelzebul, the prince of demons, that this man casts out demons'" (Matthew 12:22–24 ESV). Although the Jews accused Jesus of deriving His power from Satan, they never once failed to acknowledge His miracles; and as His staunchest opponents, they would have had every reason to dismiss them.

Life Answers

As stated in the very beginning of this chapter, miracles can be a large stumbling block for skeptics. The virgin birth, the resurrection, the healings, and the exorcisms of Jesus—in addition to many other miracles recorded in the Bible—are hindrances for some people, giving them a reason for disputing the truthfulness of God's Word. However, when we examine the evidence closely and reflect on how God's Word presents miracles, it is evident that miracles should be a stepping stone to faith rather than a stumbling block.

Points to Remember

1. Common objections to miracles are: many people have never witnessed a miracle; miracles violate the laws of nature; and only superstitious and primitive people believe in them.

2. Miracles are of a divine nature and must be expected to be extraordinary when carried out by the intervention of God in a supernatural way.

3. The laws of nature are not complete, as science still has much to discover regarding those laws.

4. God created the world and the laws of nature and can thus do with them as He chooses.

5. We cannot always discern the difference between the natural and supernatural without special revelation.

6. The Jews were a civilized people who had reason to be skeptical, and yet they believed Jesus performed miracles.

Notes

[1] William Lane Craig, "The Problem of Miracles," *Reasonable Faith* (Wheaton, IL: Crossway, 2008).

Chapter 4

Is the Bible True?

Examining the Facts about Scripture

All Scripture is God-breathed and is useful for teaching, rebuking, correcting and training in righteousness. — 2 Timothy 3:16

The Bible is the world's best seller—period. In all of recorded human history, no book has sold more copies than the Bible.[1] Yet, almost as a contradiction, no book has been hated and despised more than the Bible. The Bible communicates a powerful message about a God to whom we are accountable; and although the Bible says that salvation through Jesus Christ is available to everyone, it also describes everlasting punishment for those who reject His message.

The Bible has been the source of many movements in history, including the struggle for civil rights for all persons, the protection of life in the womb, and the sanctity of biblical marriage. It has been the source of many polarizing debates involving moral and ethical issues in every era of human history. This is one reason the Bible has been misunderstood and despised. Just as the truth of God cost John the Baptist his head for opposing Herod's marital decisions (Matthew 14:1–12), the Bible has likewise inspired believers to take stands that run counter to their culture. Even pop songs now, such as "Same Love"[2] by Macklemore and Ryan Lewis, attack the Bible as being irrelevant, ancient, and incapable of providing sound guidance to modern society. With so much controversy surrounding the Bible, it is important to know whether or not the Bible can be trusted. So, throughout this chapter, we will explore six reasons we can trust the Bible.

Reason #1: The Bible Is of Divine Origin

The first reason is that the Bible clearly claims that it is the work of God and is not of human origin. Of course, men wrote the words of the Bible, but it is God who gave them the words to write. This argument may sound like circular reasoning; so to simplify the argument, God inspired the biblical writers to record His revelation of Himself to humanity, but He allowed them to express themselves according to their own writing styles. The Bible clearly claims to be "the word of God" (Mark 7:13; 2 Corinthians 4:2; Ephesians 6:17; Hebrews 4:12), also frequently referring to itself as "the word of the Lord" (Exodus 9:20; Acts 13:44, 48–49). Several times the Bible says, "The Lord said," or "says the Lord" (Luke 18:6; Romans 12:19; 14:11); "God said . . ." (Genesis 1:3; Jonah 4:9; 1 Chronicles 11:2); "The Lord spoke/said to . . ." (Genesis 2:18; Exodus 3:7; Numbers 3:40); and "the word of the Lord came to . . ." (Genesis 15:1; 1 Samuel 15:10; 1 Kings 6:11). These are all important because they reveal that the Bible claims to express the mind of God with divine authority.

The Bible also says it is inspired by God, meaning that God inspired the writers to write His message and words. Paul wrote, "All Scripture is God-breathed [or inspired]"

(2 Timothy 3:16). The Bible claims inerrancy; that is to say, written without error, and that it is authoritative. Essentially the Bible claims this: The Bible is from God and is not of human origin; therefore, it is to be regarded as divinely inspired. If the Bible was simply of human origin, it could be filled with mistakes, professing false ideologies and promoting wrong teachings. However, because the Bible is from God, those who choose to follow Him must take Scripture as God's written revelation, pushing back against all attempts to undermine its authority. Defending the Bible is about defending the truth God has given humanity, not about defending a religious book. Paul wrote, "For what if some did not believe? Will their unbelief make the faithfulness of God without effect? Certainly not! Indeed, let God be true but every man a liar" (Romans 3:3–4 NKJV). Paul understood that God's truth must hold above every other supposed truth. Thankfully, God has provided an ample amount of evidence outside the Bible to prove His Word to be true.

Reason #2: The Bible's Message Is Unique

Comparing the message of the Bible to books of other religious systems reveals the the Bible's uniqueness. Lewis Sperry Chafer, founder of Dallas Theological Seminary, wrote, "The Bible is not such a book a man would write if he could, or could write if he would."[3]

The Bible describes a God whose attributes differ vastly from any other god recorded in history. Other gods may share certain attributes, but none possess all the attributes ascribed to God in Scripture.

The Bible reveals Jesus Christ as the God-man. Though there are instances in history of people being half-god and half-human (or a demigod) such as Hercules, there are no other instances that depict someone being fully man and fully God. This unique message in the Bible is without parallel in other religious writings.

The Bible teaches that humanity is inherently evil and sinful, worthy of God's wrath and condemnation. Other religions often teach that humanity is good, perhaps not as good as we should be, but never that humans are inherently evil, sinful, and hopeless.

The Bible teaches that punishment for sin is everlasting, conscious torment. Though other religions teach punishment for those who do not measure up to a divine standard, the punishment is not eternal and conscious, and these religions often speak of a way to be released eventually. Only the Christian Bible describes a state of perpetual punishment referred to as *hell*.

The Bible teaches that salvation is apart from works. Other religions teach that a person can attain salvation by doing enough good works. Most major religions teach the idea of scales, where a person's life is weighed with the ultimate question of salvation resting on a person's ability to do more good works than bad.

The message of the Bible contains many doctrines humans would not have written on their own without being divinely inspired to do so, because it describes humans as evil, unredeemable by our own good works, and worthy of eternal punishment if we reject God's free offer of salvation.

Finally, all religions offer a way of salvation. The way usually takes the form of a path you must walk or a set of tasks you must accomplish. The Bible teaches that the way is a person. Other religious systems point to a way of salvation, but Jesus said, "I am the way, and the truth, and the life. No one comes to the Father except through me" (John 14:6 ESV). The exclusive nature of salvation through substitutionary, divine atonement by one man sets the Bible's message of salvation apart from every other religious system. Many of the teachings that point out the exclusive nature of salvation as being attainable only through Christ are not popular because the twenty-first-century world values inclusion and diversity over everything else. However, God's Word is the final word—His revelation of Himself to those created in His image.

Reason #3: The Bible's Content Is Unified

Although the Bible was written over a long period of time, by different authors in various places, it displays a remarkably unified message. Consider the following facts.

1. The Bible was written over a period of 1,550 years. Many of the human writers did not know each other due to time and location.

2. There are forty different writers of the Bible.

3. The Bible was written in different places. For example, Moses wrote in the desert; David wrote in the countryside; Solomon wrote from a royal court; Jeremiah wrote in a dungeon; Ezekiel wrote while in exile; Daniel wrote in a pagan palace; Luke wrote while traveling; Paul wrote in prison;

and John wrote on an island. The Bible was written on three different continents (Europe, Africa, and Asia).

4. The Bible was written in three languages: Hebrew, Aramaic, and Greek.

5. The Bible was written in a variety of styles, and it reflects a variety of moods of the writers. For example, some writers wrote with ecstatic joy. Others wrote as depressed exiles, beaten down by worry. Still others wrote in peril as they ran for their lives. The Bible's subject matter is incredibly diverse. Subjects such as heaven and earth, the invisible and visible (or metaphysical), God, angels, humanity, time and eternity, life and death, sin and salvation, and heaven and hell are all subjects addressed in the Bible. Because the Bible speaks with authority, it often creates controversy.

With all of these facts—forty different people writing on controversial subjects from different places, speaking different languages, in different styles, expressing different emotions over a period of 1,550 years—the Bible should not be unified. And yet the Bible proclaims a unified truth without contradiction from Genesis all the way to Revelation and stands as an example of complete, harmonized unity. These facts alone lend great credibility to the Bible's divine inspiration.

Reason #4: The Bible Is Accurate Prophetically

The Bible is filled with prophecies. Perhaps the easiest way to disprove the Bible (if it were possible to do so) is to point out any prophecy given in the Bible and show how it failed to come true. However, these sort of prophecies are not in the Bible because, so far, all of the prophecies given by God have come true. Scripture tells of false prophets who shared false prophecies, but they were revealed to be false before their prophecies failed.[4] In fact, prophecy was taken so seriously in the Bible that prophesying falsely was punishable by death. Deuteronomy 18:20 states, "But a prophet who presumes to speak in my name anything I have not commanded, or a prophet who speaks in the name of other gods, is to be put to death." A true prophet of God would not speak unless he was sure that God had spoken to him and he was speaking God's truth.

The greatest contribution to the truth of the Bible given by prophecies, however, is the large number of prophecies that were true. Consider the following prophecies that came true in the Bible.

1. Abraham and Sarah would have a son (Genesis 15:1–6; 17:1–5; 18:1–19; 21:1–6).

2. Joseph's ten older brothers would bow to him (Genesis 37:1–11; 42:5–6).

3. A member of David's household would rebel against him (2 Samuel 12:7–12; 15; 16:21–22; 17–19).

4. Peter would deny the Lord three times (Matthew 26:31–34, 69–75).

5. Paul would witness for the Lord in Rome (Acts 23:11; 28:17–30).

6. Judah and Jerusalem were spared from the Assyrians, but fell at the hands of the Babylonians (Isaiah 39:6; Jeremiah 25:9–12).

7. The destruction of Samaria was final, but that of Jerusalem was followed by a restoration (Micah 1:6–9; Jeremiah 29:10–14).

8. The exile to Babylon would last 70 years (Jeremiah 29:10–14).

9. The name of the man (Cyrus) who issued the decree to restore Judah was predicted 150 years before he was born (Isaiah 44:28; 45:1).

10. The Medes and Persians overthrew Babylon (Isaiah 21:2; Daniel 5:28).

11. The city of Jerusalem and the temple were rebuilt (Isaiah 44:28).

These prophecies represent just a small portion of the prophecies recorded in the Bible that came true, and many of them are proven, through archaeology, to have happened historically just as the Bible predicted.

Reason #5: The Bible Is Accurate Scientifically

Contrary to popular belief, the Bible often speaks accurately to science. The church has been accused of being scientifically inaccurate, however careful consideration reveals the Bible has never been proved to be scientifically inaccurate.

Consider the following scientific facts found in the Bible preceding human "scientific discovery" of these facts.

1. The process of evaporation, condensation, and precipitation was described by Isaiah (Isaiah 55:10) and Solomon (Ecclesiastes 1:7) centuries before scientists knew how these processes work.

2. The Bible revealed the sea has paths within it (Psalm 8:8; Proverbs 8:29) well before this fact was discovered by scientists.

3. At one time, scientists believed diseases could be cured by bleeding the disease out of a person's body. Modern science now recognizes that excessive blood loss results in death. Yet the Bible stated these facts millennia ago in Leviticus 17:11, declaring that the life of a creature is in the blood.

4. Ancient theories were put forth suggesting the earth was resting on something (the back of a tortoise, the back of Hercules, etc.), yet the Bible explicitly states the earth is suspended over nothing in Job, the oldest book of the Bible (26:7).

5. Finally, people once believed that the earth is flat, yet the Bible declares in Isaiah 40:22 that the earth is round.

All of these facts point to the scientific accuracy of the Bible, lending additional credibility to its claim of truth.

Reason #6: The Historical Accuracy of the Bible Can Be Proved from Archaeology, Geology, and Eyewitness Accounts

For centuries, the Bible was thought to be filled with many fictional stories because there was no historical evidence of many of the people or places described in the Bible. For example, Nebuchadnezzar was thought to be a fictitious person until evidence surfaced in recent years that proved him to be an ancient ruler during the time and place corresponding with the biblical account of his life. The following events, people, and cultures have all been verified:

1. the flood in Noah's day

2. the destruction of Sodom and Gomorrah

3. the history of the Hebrew patriarchs

4. the fall of Jericho

5. the reign of King David

6. the accuracy of biblical statements regarding life in Israel, Egypt, Assyria, Babylon, and Medo-Persia

7. Luke's statements about thirty-two countries, fifty-four cities, nine islands, and several rulers confirmed by various archaeological findings

8. evidence of the reigns of Cyrenius, Lysanias, Paulus, and Gallio

These are just some of the evidences found that prove the Bible to be true in its historical accuracy. Evidence has been found on rock inscriptions, walls, statues, obelisks, pavement slabs, clay tablets, papyrus rolls, coins, seals, and pottery. More than five thousand archaeological findings have confirmed the Bible's historical accuracy—more than any other religion. Also, no major teaching of the Bible has been disproved by archaeological findings. The painstaking historical accuracy of the Bible should give us confidence in the truth of the Scriptures.

The overall witness of the Bible rises or falls on the dependability of the New Testament documents. The New Testament rises or falls based on the dependability of the four Gospels. Because the Gospels were written by and during the lifetime of the eyewitnesses, they are the most reliable documents we possess from the ancient world. We have more copies of the New Testament than any other book from antiquity. There are at least 5,700 copies of the New Testament in the original Greek. When you add the approximately 19,000 early translations in Old Syriac, Old Latin, Coptic, the Latin Vulgate and other languages, the grand total rises to more than 25,000 manuscripts, dating back to as early as AD 117. The most manuscripts for any other book is Homer's *Iliad* with just 643 manuscripts. We know that the Synoptic Gospels (Matthew, Mark, and Luke) were written and being circulated as early as AD 60. When you take into account the fact Jesus was crucified circa AD 33, that means the Gospels were written and being circulated during the lifetime of the eyewitnesses.

Finally, we know the New Testament is reliable because of the confirmation of the manuscripts by the early church fathers. Justin Martyr, Irenaeus, Clement of Alexandria,

Origen, Tertullian, Hippolytus, Polycarp, and many others provided at least 19,368 citations of the text of the Gospels alone. Since all of these early church leaders lived within the time frame of the first Christian century, we have proof that the New Testament was being circulated and quoted as the standard for orthodox faith shortly after it was written.

All of the important facts recorded in the Gospels about Jesus's life are backed up by the historical testimony of Tacitus, Suetonius, Thallus, Josephus, Pliny the Elder, and the Jewish Talmud. The following eleven facts about Jesus's life and the early church are established and universally accepted from information provided by the above listed historians:

1. Jesus was from Nazareth.

2. He lived a virtuous life.

3. He performed unusual feats.

4. He introduced new teaching that contradicted elements of Judaism.

5. He was crucified under Pontius Pilate.

6. His disciples believed He rose from the dead.

7. His disciples denied polytheism and proclaimed monotheism.

8. His disciples worshipped Him.

9. His teaching and the number of His disciples spread rapidly.

10. His followers had no fear of death.

11. His followers renounced material goods.

No book from antiquity has a smaller gap between the original and the first existing manuscript copy. The earliest undisputed manuscript is a fragment of the Gospel of John known as John Ryland's Papyrus. It dates somewhere between AD 177 and 138. Entire New Testament books, including a Gospel and some of the Epistles, were found in the Bodmer Papyri, which dates to AD 200, and most of the New Testament is available in the Chester Beatty Papyri dating back to AD 250.

Life Answers

Though the Bible is hotly contested by many people as irrelevant, false, and antiquated, the Bible has proved time and time again that it can be trusted.

Points to Remember

1. The Bible claims to have originated from God, rather than humans.

2. The Bible has a unique message that is not found in any other religious text, thus separating itself from any man-made institution.

3. Though written over many centuries with multiple authors and in various locations, the Bible demonstrates a unified message.

4. The prophetic accuracy in the Bible lends credibility to the truth of Scripture.

5. The scientific accuracy in the Bible lends credibility to the truth of Scripture.

6. The historical accuracy lends credibility to the truth of Scripture, as no other religious text can claim historical accuracy over such a broad time period regarding so many locations, cultures, and people.

7. The number of New Testament manuscripts, the eyewitness accounts of the manuscripts, and the witness of the early church fathers combine together to present irrefutable evidence that the Bible can be trusted to be much more accurate than any other ancient document.

Notes

[1] "Best-selling Book of Non-fiction," Guiness World Records, accessed March 1, 2018, http://www.guinnessworldrecords.com/world-records /best-selling-book-of-non-fiction.

[2] "Same Love," written by Ben Haggerty, Mary Lambert, and Ryan Lewis (Kobalt Music Publishing, 2012). See http://songmeanings.com/songs /view/3530822107859436563/.

[3] Quoted by Josh McDowell, in *Evidence that Demands a Verdict* (San Bernardino, CA: Campus Crusade for Christ, 1972), 25.

[4] See Story of Jehoshaphat in 1 Kings 22.

Chapter 5

Who Is Jesus Christ?

How Do We Know Jesus Existed?

The Word became flesh and made his dwelling among us. We have seen his glory, the glory of the one and only Son, who came from the Father, full of grace and truth. — John 1:14

Jesus Christ is the most influential person in history. Napoleon Bonaparte, one of the most successful and notorious emperors and conquerors in history, had this to say about Jesus: "Alexander, Caesar, Charlemagne, and myself have founded great empires, but on what did those creations of our genius rest? Upon force. But Jesus founded his on love. This very day millions would die for him. . . . I think I understand something of human nature, and I tell you, all these were men, and I am a man. Jesus Christ was more than man."[1]

More than two thousand years have passed since Jesus Christ's time on earth, and yet there are still people who willingly die for His name. As I write, the terrorist group known as ISIS is spreading terror by beheading Christians, videoing their gruesome deaths, and publishing them online. But these Christians are choosing to die rather than deny the name of Christ. While their senseless deaths at the hands of barbarians horrify us, their love, devotion, and complete level of surrender serves as an inspiration to everyone who claims the name of Christ. Throughout human history people have died for their country, their leader, or for a shared cause; but in Christ alone we find people who are willing to die for someone who died over two centuries ago. The difference is, Jesus is more than just an inspiring leader or one who possessed a unique idea. He is the risen, living Savior, who, through the presence and power of the Holy Spirit, inspires people of every age all over the world.

There are more poems, songs, and books written about Jesus than any other person or subject. His entrance into human history divided history into two parts: events that took place before Jesus came to earth (BC) and events that took place after Jesus came to earth (AD). Jesus is, without dispute, the most influential person ever to live on this earth. And He is alive today!

While the preceding statement is undeniably true, it is controversial. So, if Jesus is the most influential person who ever lived, then who is He, and why is He so influential? This question explores Jesus's identity and earthly mission. Some say He was a great teacher or an exceptionally gifted prophet. Others say He was the prophesied Messiah of the Jewish Scriptures (the Old Testament), and most Christians today believe Him to be fully God and fully man. Understanding Jesus Christ is essential to understanding His purpose and influence.

A good Christian apologetic argument must address those who make the case that Jesus is a mythical figure no different from Hercules or Peter Pan. Over the past one hundred years there has been a significant increase in the number of scholars who question the veracity and accuracy of the entire New Testament. Many of these scholars have gone so far as to suggest the New Testament is an elaborate myth, invented by the church to gain control over the lives of believers. Therefore, the existence of the historical Jesus is called into question. Obviously, Christianity hangs on the person and work of Jesus Christ, so any philosophy or teaching that would seriously call His existence into question must be addressed by presenting the historical evidence that Jesus Christ lived.

Who Is Jesus?

Jesus carried many names and titles during His time on earth. He was called Jesus, Christ, Messiah, God, Son of God, Son of Man, and many more names. Yet, to get the most accurate picture of who Jesus really is, we will begin by examining how His contemporaries saw Him.

Jesus is the Christ, or Messiah. Jesus, when speaking to the Pharisees one day referred to Himself as the Christ.

> Now while the Pharisees were gathered together, Jesus asked them a question, saying, "What do you think about the Christ? Whose son is he?" They said to him, "The son of David." He said to them, "How is it then that David, in the Spirit, calls him Lord, saying,
>
> 'The Lord said to my Lord,
> "Sit at my right hand,
>   until I put your enemies under your feet"'?
>
> If then David calls him Lord, how is he his son?"
>   (Matthew 22:41–45 ESV)

Jesus referred to Himself here as the Christ, or the Messiah. Jewish leaders would have known the Messiah would be a "son of David," so Jesus's reference in this passage would be an affirmation that He is the promised Messiah. The Christ, or Messiah, would ultimately save God's people and establish a new Kingdom. Jesus came to do just that, and one day, He will return as King.

Jesus's encounter with the woman at the well at Sychar, recorded in John 4, is another example of Jesus's affirmation that He is the promised Messiah. At one point in the encounter the woman says to Jesus, "I know that Messiah is coming (He who is called Christ); when that One comes, He will declare all things to us." Jesus replies, "I who speak to you am He" (verses 25–26 NASB). Scripture further establishes the connection between Jesus and the messianic prophecies of the Old Testament in Luke 4:16–21. In this passage, Jesus enters the synagogue in Nazareth on the Sabbath and stands up to read from Scripture. He is handed the scroll of the prophet Isaiah, which He unrolls and begins reading.

> "The Spirit of the Lord is on me,
>   because he has anointed me
>   to proclaim good news to the poor.
> He has sent me to proclaim freedom for the
>   prisoners
>   and recovery of sight for the blind,
> to set the oppressed free,
>   to proclaim the year of the Lord's favor."
>   (verses 18–19).

He then, very calmly, rolls up the scroll, hands it back to the attendant, sits down, and says, "Today this scripture is fulfilled in your hearing" (verse 21). That last statement would have been a theological bombshell for those who were listening. Jesus has just read from Isaiah 61, which everyone would have recognized as a messianic prophecy. He then says this prophecy is fulfilled today because He has come and His ministry has begun.

Throughout the New Testament, Jesus is also often referred to as the Savior. When Jesus was born, the announcement of His birth included the title, Savior. Luke 2 says, "For there is born to you this day in the city of David a Savior, who is Christ the Lord" (verse 11 NKJV). When Paul first began preaching, he included this in his message in Acts 13:23, "From this man's descendants God has brought to Israel the Savior Jesus, as he promised." Jesus Himself said in Luke 19:10 that He came to seek and save the lost. Jesus's sinless life, His selfless sacrifice on the cross, and His glorious resurrection are all fulfillments of the mission of the Savior of the world. As previously mentioned, the woman at the well of Sychar not only heard Jesus proclaim Himself to be the long-awaited Messiah, she also proclaimed Him to be the Savior of the world. The people of Sychar, hearing her testimony and hearing Jesus's own words agreed, saying, "It is no longer because of what you said that we believe, for we have heard for ourselves and know that this One is indeed the Savior of the world" (John 4:42–43 NASB).

Jesus, as Savior, is affirmed by the early preaching of the apostles in the book of Acts. Acts 5 records that the apostles were arrested and imprisoned by the high priest and Sadducees for preaching the gospel. But an angel of the Lord appeared that night and set them free, so they were found preaching the gospel again the very next day. Being brought before the council again, they were forbidden to preach the truth about Jesus. "But Peter and the apostles answered, 'We must obey God rather than men. The God of our fathers raised Jesus, whom you killed by hanging him on a tree. God exalted him at his right hand as Leader and Savior'" (Acts 5:29–31 ESV). From Jesus's birth, to His death, to the early preaching of the apostles, Jesus proclaimed Himself and was known and proclaimed by others as the Savior of the world.

Jesus is also the Son of God. He referred to Himself as the Son of God in many places throughout the New Testament. For example, He said, "This illness does not lead to death. It is for the glory of God, so that the Son of God may be glorified through it" (John 11:4 ESV).[2] Jesus was proclaimed as the Son of God by the demonic forces that He had forever defeated (Mark 3:11). His disciples recognized Him as the Son of God (Matthew 14:33; 16:16). He was recognized by Gentiles as the Son of God (Mark 15:39). And the angel Gabriel announced to Mary that the child that would be born to her would be the Son of God (Luke 1:35). Jesus is also commonly referred to as the Son of God by the apostles in both Acts and the Epistles. Paul included this in his opening of the letter to the Romans, "[Jesus], who was descended from David according to the flesh and was declared to be the Son of God in power according to the Spirit of holiness by his resurrection from the dead" (1:3–4 ESV). The miracle of being part of God's family is extended to us as He invites us to be adopted as sons and daughters of God. Paul explained that Jesus is the first, unique Son (Colossians 1:15); but because we have been grafted into the vine (Romans 11:17–19) and adopted into His family (8:15), John wrote that we can now "be called children of God" (1 John 3:1).

The most common name used in the Gospels for Jesus is Son of Man. Jesus referred to Himself by this name more than seventy times in the Gospels. *Son of Man* means the "ideal man" or the "representative man." By using this term Christ usually showed the part of Himself that was human. For example, His humility is demonstrated in Matthew 8:20 when He said, "Foxes have dens and birds have nests, but the Son of Man has no place to lay his head." He used this term to refer to Himself as a servant. "The Son of Man did not come to be served, but to serve, and to give his life as a ransom for many" (20:28). Jesus also used it to depict His pain and suffering. "As you know, the Passover is two days away—and the Son of Man will be handed over to be crucified" (26:2).[3] All of these times when Jesus referred to Himself as the Son of Man, His humanity was revealed.

However, there is also a messianic connection to the title "Son of Man" that comes from the book of Daniel. In the first half of Daniel 7, the prophet recorded a dream, which in part raises the messianic connection of Jesus to the title Son of Man. Daniel wrote,

> "I was watching in the night visions,
> And behold, One like the Son of Man,
> Coming with the clouds of heaven!
> He came to the Ancient of Days,
> And they brought Him near before Him.
> Then to Him was given dominion and glory and a
>   kingdom,

> That all the peoples, nations, and languages
>   should serve Him.
> His dominion is an everlasting dominion,
> Which shall not pass away,
> And His kingdom the one
> Which shall not be destroyed." (verses 13–14 NKJV)

Clearly, this is a reference to the coming Messiah, who will ultimately rule and reign over a Kingdom that will not pass away. Most Jews would know that when Jesus used the title Son of Man, He was referring to Himself as the promised Messiah of the Hebrew Scriptures.

Hopefully, you now have a better understanding of who Jesus said He really is, so the only question remaining is whether or not Jesus actually exists.

Did Jesus Exist Historically?

Biblical Sources

When most people ask you to prove that Jesus existed on the earth, they are typically asking if there is any evidence other than the Bible. Yet, before moving on to extrabiblical sources, we must understand that the Bible is the most valuable source attesting to Jesus's existence.[4] The New Testament contains four Gospels, an account of the apostles' activities after Jesus's ascension, and multiple letters written by eyewitnesses to the life, teaching, ministry, death, and resurrection of Jesus. Every single account treats Jesus as a real person. However, can the Gospels be trusted as accurate? Absolutely!

The New Testament is actually one of the best preserved documents in history. There are more copies of the New Testament than any other ancient manuscript—and it leads by thousands.

Some scholars attack the dating of the New Testament. They acknowledge the many copies, yet they argue that the Gospel accounts were written more than a century, if not centuries, after Jesus walked the earth. Many conclude that this would mean Jesus did not exist. However, Matthew, Mark, and Luke (otherwise known as the Synoptic Gospels) are all dated before AD 70. This is important because Jerusalem was destroyed in AD 70, yet these Gospels demonstrate a thorough knowledge and understanding of Jerusalem before its destruction. According to New Testament scholar, Craig Evans, other gospels that have been written, such as the gospel of Thomas or Peter, can unwittingly ignore certain customs or traditions that would have been known to anyone who lived in Jerusalem during that time.[5] For example, the writer of the gospel of Peter was not aware of Jewish burial customs or impurity rituals that anyone who lived in Jerusalem during the time of Jesus would have known. Thus, the cultural accuracy of the Gospels allows for a dating before AD 70, which means that these three Gospels[6] were written within a few years after Jesus's death. Both the Gospels and Epistles also contain idioms that are consistent with the Hebrew and Syriac idioms of the times in which Jesus lived.[7] All of this information lends credibility to the Gospels and the New Testament as a useful, accurate, and historical source that proves the existence of Jesus.

Extrabiblical Sources

In addition to the Bible, plenty of other sources confirm Jesus's existence. Flavius Josephus, one of the most famous Jewish historians who wrote during the time of Jesus, acknowledged that Jesus was a real person.

> Now, there was about this time Jesus, a wise man, if it be lawful to call him a man, for he was a doer of wonderful works, a teacher of such men as receive the truth with pleasure. He drew over to him both many of the Jews, and many of the Gentiles. He was the Christ. And when Pilate, at the suggestion of the principal men amongst us, had condemned him to the cross, those that loved him at the first did not forsake him; for he appeared to them alive again on the third day; as the divine prophets had foretold these and thousand other wonderful things concerning him.[8]

Josephus, who was Jewish, would have had reason to dismiss Christ as an authentic person of history, but he was compelled to include Him as a real person who lived in Jerusalem during the time the Gospels proclaim His life and ministry.

A Roman historian, Tacitus, also wrote of Jesus as a genuine historical figure. He wrote that Jesus was executed under Pontius Pilate during the Roman reign of Tiberius. Another Roman, Suetonius, chief secretary to Emperor Hadrian, wrote that there was a man named *Christos* (or Christ) who lived during the first century.

The Jewish Babylonian Talmud also mentions Jesus as a historical figure. Though it accuses Him of being born out of wedlock and of blasphemy, it nevertheless acknowledges Him as a real person.

More Evidence

Perhaps the most convincing evidence for the existence of Jesus is the existence of the church. If Jesus never lived as a real person, it seems unlikely that the church would have lasted without being revealed as a hoax. Of course, someone may have fabricated the story of Jesus in later centuries and claimed it to be history. Yet, this is highly unlikely, since the Synoptic Gospels predate the fall of Jerusalem, and since there is an extensive historical record of Christianity in its early stages during the first century. If the story were fabricated it would have been fabricated during the first century; but Christianity threatened the Jewish religion to the extent that it would not have endured if it had been a hoax. If there is no Jesus, then there can be no Christianity. The beginning of Christianity itself is a testament to the real existence of Jesus Christ.

Life Answers

Though there is much confusion about Jesus, we can be assured that Jesus was a real person and that He is who He said He is because of the evidence from first-century writers and historians, whether biblical or extrabiblical. Scholar Gottfried Less "concludes that there is no more reason to doubt that the Gospels come from the traditional authors than there is to doubt that the works of Philo or Josephus are authentic, *except* that the Gospels contain supernatural events."[9] Since the existence of Jesus can be proved, then His claims must be taken seriously!

Points to Remember

1. Jesus is the Christ.

2. Jesus is the Savior.

3. Jesus is the Son of God.

4. Jesus is the Son of Man.

5. The New Testament and accounts of the existence of Jesus can be verified historically.

6. Non-Christian historians such as Josephus and Tacitus account for Jesus's existence.

7. The existence of Christianity and the existence of the church from the first century until now provide reason for the existence of Jesus.

Notes

[1] Michael Green, "What Makes Jesus So Special Then?" *But Don't All Religions Lead to God?* (Grand Rapids, MI: Baker, 2002), 28–29.

[2] See also Matthew 26:63–64; Luke 22:70; John 3:16–17; 5:25–26; 10:36–38.

[3] See also Matthew 20:18–19; John 3:14–15.

[4] Refer back to Chapter 4 for more information on why the Bible can be trusted.

[5] Lee Strobel, "Challenge #1." *The Case for the Real Jesus* (Grand Rapids, MI: Zondervan, 2007), loc. 438, Kindle.

[6] Most scholars believe that John wrote his Gospel toward the end of his life in AD 90–100.

[7] William Lane Craig, "The Resurrection of Jesus," *Reasonable Faith* (Wheaton, IL: Crossway, 2008), 334.

[8] Flavius Josephus, "Antiquities of the Jews," *The Complete Works of Flavius Josephus* (Green Forest, AR: New Leaf, 2008), 426

[9] Craig, "The Resurrection of Jesus," 334.

Chapter 6

Did the Resurrection Really Happen?

The Historical Evidence that Jesus Died and Rose from the Dead

For what I received I passed on to you as of first importance: that Christ died for our sins according to the Scriptures, that he was buried, that he was raised on the third day according to the Scriptures, and that he appeared to Cephas, and then to the Twelve. — 1 Corinthians 15:3–5

Now if Christ is proclaimed as raised from the dead, how can some of you say that there is no resurrection of the dead? But if there is no resurrection of the dead, then not even Christ has been raised. And if Christ has not been raised, then our preaching is in vain and your faith is in vain. We are even found to be misrepresenting God, because we testified about God that he raised Christ, whom he did not raise if it is true that the dead are not raised. For if the dead are not raised, not even Christ has been raised. And if Christ has not been raised, your faith is futile and you are still in your sins. Then those also who have fallen asleep in Christ have perished. If in Christ we have hope in this life only, we are of all people most to be pitied. (1 Corinthians 15:12–19 ESV)

These verses demonstrate how vital the resurrection is to the Christian faith. Paul proclaimed that the Christian faith hangs on the truth of the resurrection of Jesus Christ. If the resurrection is not true, then Christianity is a fraud. The veracity and believability of the world's largest religion rests solely upon the validity of the resurrection. While this is true, we must also realize it is not just Christianity as a world religion that rests upon the resurrection; it is our personal hope in eternal life that is dependent on the resurrection of the Lord Jesus Christ. The Bible teaches that anyone who sincerely believes upon the Lord Jesus Christ will resurrect in the last day only because Jesus Christ resurrected first (1 Corinthians 15:23). Therefore, not only would the institution of Christianity crumble if the resurrection proved to be false, but our eternal hope would lay crumbled beside the remains of a discredited religion.

Jesus would have to be considered a liar if He did not rise from the grave because He predicted His resurrection several times. Mark 9:31 reads, "[Jesus] said to [his disciples], 'The Son of Man is going to be delivered into the hands of men. They will kill him, and after three days He will rise.'"[1] If the resurrection of Christ cannot be trusted, the entire Bible would be rightly called into question since the resurrection is the cornerstone of the Christian faith.

As we have noted, there is much at stake for Christianity if the resurrection is not true. Critics of Christianity realize the critical role the resurrection plays in our faith, and they seek every opportunity to undermine the evidence for the resurrection. There have been attempts in recent years to claim that Jesus's bones have been found in Jerusalem.

In 2007 Dr. James Tabor, Hollywood director James Cameron, and filmmaker Simcha Jacobovici teamed up to produce a pseudo-documentary for the Discovery Channel on the so-called, "Jesus Tomb."[2] The documentary claimed the Talpiot Tomb, discovered in the old city of Jerusalem in 1980, contained the names "Jesus, son of Joseph," Maria (or Mary), Matia (or Matthew), Mariamne Mara, (which, they claimed was Mary Magdalene), and "Judah, son of Jesus." The documentary claims, based on the evidence found in the tomb, Jesus did not rise from the dead but married Mary Magdalene, had a son, then died and was buried with His family in the Talpiot Tomb.

The scope of this study does not allow for detailed refutation of the claims associated with the Talpiot Tomb, but the words of the archaeologists who worked on the excavation of the tomb should be sufficient. Amos Kloner, the archaeologist who oversaw the tomb's excavation said, "The possibility of it [the tomb] being Jesus' family [is] very close to zero."[3] All of the other archaeologists who worked on the project, including Motti Neiger of the Israeli Antiquities Authority agreed the chances of this tomb being Jesus's family tomb are "almost nil."[4] So whenever a sensational claim such as this one is made, the claim is found to be a hoax or evidentially false. But the claims should be taken seriously and thoroughly investigated because the truth of God's Word can withstand the attacks leveled against it.

Though the death of Jesus fulfilled the law and provided atonement for our sins, the resurrection is ultimately where our hope is grounded. We are forgiven of our sins through the blood Jesus shed on the cross, but the validity of His sacrifice is proved in His resurrection. So let's take an honest look at the evidence for the resurrection of Jesus.

The Empty Tomb

The first piece of evidence is perhaps the most basic and simple—the empty tomb. If the tomb was really empty, and no natural explanation can be provided to explain why it was empty, then Jesus was indeed resurrected. Many scholars and nonbelievers actually agree that the tomb was empty, but they object to the resurrection by stating there are natural explanations as to why it was empty.

One of the more popular natural explanations of the empty tomb of Jesus Christ states that the women who discovered the empty tomb simply went to the wrong tomb. Somehow, these women, faithful followers of Jesus who likely visited the tomb on the day Jesus was buried, went to the wrong tomb the third day. Explanations for this range from they were confused, to they misidentified the tomb in the low light of the early morning. Another explanation says they were so overcome with grief they mistakenly went to the wrong tomb. If this is true, consider the implications that must logically follow this claim. First, the disciples who checked the tomb after the women reported it to be empty, must also have gone to the wrong tomb. It is highly unlikely the disciples would have gone to the wrong tomb to verify the women's story without realizing their mistake. Further implications of this claim would also mean that the Roman and Jewish officials would have checked the wrong tomb as well. In reality, there are too many people who would have had to consecutively check the wrong tomb for this hypothesis to be true.

Another popular explanation suggests the disciples came in the night and stole Jesus's body from the tomb. Many persons throughout history have claimed that Jesus's body was stolen and hidden or destroyed by His disciples to fake His resurrection. There is an abundance of evidence disproving this theory. In Jewish culture during the time of Jesus's death, a story claiming such an important event would not have involved women as the ones who discovered the empty tomb because of their diminished roles in the patriarchal society during the time period. If the story of the resurrection was fabricated, the disciples would not have cast women in the role of discovering the empty tomb—especially Mary Magdalene who had once been possessed by demons.

The "disciples moved the body" theory has another serious problem. The Bible records that Roman guards were posted outside of the tomb. The Jewish leaders feared Jesus's body would be stolen because they knew that He predicted He would rise from the dead in three days. The Jews were concerned that Jesus's disciples would come and steal His body and claim He had been resurrected. Matthew 27:62–66 says:

> The next day, the one after Preparation Day, the chief priests and the Pharisees went to Pilate. "Sir," they said, "we remember that while he was still alive that deceiver said, 'After three days I will rise again.' So give the order for the tomb to be made secure until the third day. Otherwise, his disciples may come and steal the body and tell

the people that he has been raised from the dead. This last deception will be worse than the first."

"Take a guard," Pilate answered. "Go, make the tomb as secure as you know how." So they went and made the tomb secure by putting a seal on the stone and posting the guard.

The penalty for failing in guard duty was death.[5] The Roman guard would not have allowed the disciples into the tomb. The theft of Jesus's body was such a concern to the Jews, they took painstaking lengths to ensure that His body would remain where it was buried; and it is highly unlikely a band of fishermen, a tax collector, and other assorted non-military types would be able to overpower a contingent of trained Roman guards.

Ten of Jesus's original twelve disciples were martyred for their faith in Christ as the risen Messiah. The eleventh, John (Judas, being the twelfth), was tortured and exiled to the island of Patmos. The possibility that all of these men agreed to be tortured and killed for what they knew to be a hoax is not convincing. The disciples knew that Jesus rose from the grave, and because of this, they were willing to give their lives rather than deny this truth. Concerning the disciples' willingness to suffer torture and death to defend the resurrection, former Nixon aide turned apologist Chuck Colson said, "I know the resurrection is a fact, and Watergate proved it to me. How? Because 12 men testified they had seen Jesus raised from the dead, then they proclaimed that truth for 40 years, never once denying it. . . . Watergate embroiled 12 of the most powerful people in the world—and they couldn't keep a lie for three weeks. You're telling me 12 apostles could keep a lie for 40 years? Absolutely impossible."[6] Think about it this way. The fact the disciples chose death rather than deny that Jesus is the Christ doesn't prove Jesus is the Christ. What it proves is the disciples believed He was the Christ, and they were in the best position to know the truth. People will suffer torture and ultimately die for something they believe to be true, but they will not suffer torture and ultimately die for something they know to be false.

A final popular but implausible natural explanation for the resurrection of Jesus is referred to as the swoon theory. This theory states Jesus never died but only fainted from exhaustion and appeared to be dead. When He was placed in the coolness of the tomb, He revived, moved the stone away from the entrance, and appeared to His disciples. This theory has some very obvious shortfalls. First, the Roman guards who crucified Jesus were trained extensively in the area of crucifixion, and they would never risk the possibility of a victim surviving the cross. The fact that Jesus was scourged and beaten to a bloody pulp would certainly be enough to kill Him, but then you have to add the fact the soldiers thrust a spear into His side to make sure He was dead. Multiple medical experts have concluded the biblical account of the spear would have verified that Jesus died on the cross. John, in his account of the crucifixion records, "But one of the soldiers pierced his side with a spear, and at once there came out blood and water" (John 19:34 ESV). Because of the beating and physical torture of the cross, Jesus suffered both pericardial and pleural effusion. In other words, fluid collected in the pericardial sack around His heart and in His lungs. When the soldier pierced His side, the spear passed through

Jesus's lung and into the pericardial sack of the heart, releasing the blood and collected fluid. This proves Jesus was dead while He was on the cross. Also, because the time of the Passover observance was quickly approaching, the Jews wanted those being crucified to have their deaths hastened so they would not be on the cross when Passover began. To insure a swift death, the Roman guards broke the legs of those being crucified with Jesus (so they could not continue to push their bodies up to breathe), but they did not break Jesus's legs. Again, John recorded, "But when they came to Jesus and saw that he was already dead, they did not break his legs" (John 19:33 ESV).

The Bible says that Jesus appeared to Mary and Martha just three days after His crucifixion. After enduring the torture and pain He experienced, there is no way Jesus could have appeared as the risen victor over the grave if He had only swooned. He would have looked like someone at the point of death who needed assistance just to walk.

The Post-Resurrection Witnesses

The empty tomb is certainly sufficient evidence that Jesus's body was resurrected, but the question could have remained, where is He? Thankfully, there were many witnesses to Jesus's post-resurrection appearances that help to prove He did indeed rise from the dead. Here is a list of those witnesses:

1. Jesus appeared to Peter (1 Corinthians 15:5).
2. Jesus appeared to the twelve disciples (1 Corinthians 15:5).

3. Jesus appeared to more than five hundred people (1 Corinthians 15:6).

4. Jesus appeared to James (1 Corinthians 15:7).

5. Jesus appeared to all of the apostles (1 Corinthians 15:7).

6. Jesus appeared to Paul (1 Corinthians 15:8; Acts 9:3–7).

7. Jesus appeared to Mary Magdalene, Mary (mother of Jesus), and Salome (Matthew 28:9; Mark 16:9; John 20:11–18).

8. Jesus appeared to the two disciples on the road to Emmaus (Luke 24:13–32).

This list includes hundreds of people, but it still may not include all the people that saw Jesus after He rose from the grave.

Just as critics offer alternative theories of why the tomb was empty, they also offer alternative but highly implausible theories to explain Jesus's appearances to His disciples. One theory suggests that Jesus's post-resurrection appearance was a hallucination. But the fact hundreds of people saw the resurrected Christ at the same time makes this theory impossible. We know there have been instances of mass hallucination, where hundreds, even thousands of people have hallucinated at the same time, but they each have their own hallucination. It is not possible for hundreds of people to have the same hallucination at the same time!

Another fact to consider is that the resurrection of Jesus was physical, and Jesus appeared to His disciples in a physical form. We know this from the famous encounter Thomas had with Jesus that was recorded by the apostle John. "Then he said to Thomas, 'Put your finger here, and see my hands; and put out your hand, and place it in my side. Do not disbelieve, but believe'" (John 20:27 ESV). Jesus was not a ghost, disembodied spirit, or the product of the overactive imaginations of His disciples. He was, and is, the physically risen Christ who is now seated at the right hand of God the Father.

It is clear the resurrection of Jesus Christ was a fact in Jerusalem. Even Jesus's opponents who crucified Him did not deny the resurrection. Paul Althaus says, "The resurrection . . . could not have been maintained in Jerusalem for a single day, for a single hour, if the emptiness of the tomb had not been established as a fact for all concerned."[7] In other words, Jesus was opposed by so many people in Jerusalem, if He had not risen from the dead, His opponents would have gone to any length to dispel the story. Yet they could not refute the resurrection of the Lord Jesus Christ because it actually happened.

The Beginning of the Church

The last evidence to consider regarding the resurrection is the beginning of the Christian church. As stated at the beginning of this chapter, the resurrection is the hope of Christianity. A resurrected Savior is what sets Christianity apart from any other religion. But without the resurrection, Christianity implodes. The beginning of the New Testament church could not have happened without the truth of the resurrection. The resurrection was never in dispute by the early church. Though circumcision and food rituals were discussed, the death and resurrection of Jesus Christ formed a shared foundation of faith for all believers. Most Christians set aside Sunday for corporate worship, replacing the Sabbath, which was observed and celebrated on Saturday (Acts 20:7). They did this because Christ rose on the first day of the week, and they wanted to celebrate the resurrection on the first day of each week.

Life Answers

When taken together, the evidence for the resurrection is overwhelming. Christians can absolutely take hope in the resurrection of Jesus Christ. Let us rejoice with the apostle Peter in saying, "This Jesus God raised up again, to which we all are witnesses. . . . Therefore let all the house of Israel know for certain that God has made Him both Lord and Christ—this Jesus whom you crucified" (Acts 2:32, 36 NASB).

Points to Remember

1. The entire foundation of Christianity rests upon the truth of the resurrection.

2. The empty tomb proves that Jesus rose from the dead.

3. The willing martyrdom of the early followers of Jesus proves they believed Him to be the risen Lord of glory.

4. The many witnesses that Jesus saw after He was resurrected prove that He rose again.

5. The beginning of the Christian church and the fact the church changed its day of worship from Saturday, the

Sabbath, to the first day of the week to coincide with the day of Jesus's resurrection proves first-century Christians believed Jesus rose from the grave on the first day of the week.

Notes

1 See also Matthew 17:9; Mark 8:31; 10:32–34; 14:28; John 2:19, 21.

2 James Cameron, *The Lost Tomb of Jesus*, directed by Simcha Jacobovici, aired March 4, 2007 on The Discovery Channel.

3 James D. Tabor, *The Jesus Dynasty* (New York: Simon & Schuster), 25–26.

4 Ibid.

5 Josh McDowell, "Can You Keep a Good Man Down?" *More Than a Carpenter* (Wheaton, IL: Tyndale House, 1977), 92.

6 Colson Center (@ColsonCenter), "I know the resurrection is a fact and Watergate proved it to me. How?" Twitter, April 16, 2017, 5:47 p.m., https://twitter.com/colsoncenter/status/853771971661901825?lang =en.

7 Paul Althaus, quoted in Wolfhart Pannenberg, *Jesus—God and Man*, 2nd ed., trans. Lewis L. Wilkins and Duane A. Priebe (Philadelphia: Westminster Press, 1977), 100.

Chapter 7

What Is Salvation?

How Can a Person Be Saved?

Therefore [Jesus] is able to save completely those who come to God through him, because he always lives to intercede for them.
— Hebrews 7:25

One of the most popular words in the Christian world is *salvation*. Every Sunday, this word is mentioned millions of times in churches around the world. It is the essential core of Christianity that explains the purpose of Christ's coming to earth. Since we now know that Jesus was a real person who existed and that His resurrection really did happen, we must take His claims seriously. Inarguably, Jesus's greatest claim is summed up by His words in Luke 19:10, "For the Son of Man came to seek and to save the lost." The salvation that Jesus provides is for all who believe in Him.

This chapter explores salvation so that we may have a better understanding of what salvation is and how it can be attained. Because we know salvation is what assures us of heaven, we must be sure our understanding of salvation lines up with the revealed Word of God. By the conclusion of the chapter, we will know much more about what the Bible teaches about salvation and how it applies to our life.

The Definition of Salvation

The word *salvation* can mean different things in the Bible. The first definition of salvation can simply mean to rescue or deliver. Oftentimes this implies a physical rescue or deliverance from an enemy, affliction, or other dangers. One example of this kind of deliverance can be found in Exodus 14, immediately after the Israelites escape from the Egyptians: "Thus the LORD saved Israel that day from the hand of the Egyptians, and Israel saw the Egyptians dead on the seashore" (verse 30 NASB). The type of saving God did on that day was a physical salvation of the Hebrews from the Egyptians. Similarly, when Jesus walked on water in Matthew 14, He called for Peter to step out of the boat and join Him. The Bible says that Peter walked on the water until he noticed the storm: "But when [Peter] saw the wind, he was afraid and, beginning to sink, cried out, 'Lord, save me!'" (verse 30). Again, the type of saving Peter was calling out for was a physical rescue from a life-threatening situation.

Although this physical form of salvation is mentioned frequently in the Bible, this is not the type on which we will focus in this chapter. We will discuss a salvation that deals with a much more serious issue than one that simply saves from physical danger. True salvation in the spiritual sense is one that delivers people from sin. The whole reason that Jesus came to earth is to make possible this type of salvation. Matthew recorded, "[Mary] will bear a son, and you shall call his name Jesus, for he will save his people from their sins" (Matthew 1:21 ESV). John also captured Jesus's purpose well in his first epistle: "And we have seen and testify that the Father has sent his Son to be the Savior of the world" (1 John 4:14). These descriptions offer a window of insight into the purpose of Jesus coming to earth. He came to provide for our pardon and remove all sin guilt from us so that we can be made righteous! Or, as Paul so eloquently described it, "For our sake he made him to be sin who knew no sin, so that in him we might become the righteousness of God" (2 Corinthians 5:21 ESV).

The Need for Salvation

Humanity's greatest need is for salvation. Though human beings do not always realize this and may prioritize physical or material needs above God's salvation, salvation is infinitely more important from an eternal perspective. Jesus asks, "For what will it profit a man if he gains the whole world and forfeits his soul?" (Matthew 16:26 ESV). Though there are many things that appear to be important, and many things culture points to as important, Jesus boldly tells all who have ears to hear that a person has truly gained nothing if he loses his soul in the end. The salvation of the soul is our greatest need!

There are two basic facts that contribute to the need for salvation. First, God is *holy*. To be holy means to be sanctified or set apart. In this sense, it means that God is perfect in every way and that any evil or sin cannot come from Him. He is far removed from sin, and the nature of His holiness makes it impossible for Him to sin. Habakkuk, speaking to God said, "Your eyes are too pure to look on evil; /

you cannot tolerate wrongdoing" (Habakkuk 1:13). Though God's holiness is worthy of our praise, His holiness becomes a problem for humanity, which leads to the second basic fact: humanity is sinful.

Human beings are far from holy, and we are sinful by nature. Isaiah wrote,

> But we are all like an unclean thing,
> And all our righteousnessess are like filthy rags;
> We all fade as a leaf,
> And our iniquities, like the wind,
> Have taken us away. (Isaiah 64:6 NKJV)

Paul also wrote in Romans 3,

> "None is righteous, no, not one;
>   no one understands;
>   no one seeks for God.
> All have turned aside; together they have become
>   worthless;
>   no one does good,
>   not even one." (Romans 3:10–12 ESV)

Both of these passages support the truth that humanity is sinful!

The fact that humanity is not holy but sinful presents a problem. Though God's holiness is wonderful and is worthy to be praised, it also creates a barrier for humans. How can human beings fellowship with God if God is absolutely holy and human beings are absolutely sinful? How can God forgive humans of our sin and still be just? Isaiah said that our sin has separated us from God, and if we die separated from God we will be separated from Him forever (Isaiah 53:6). This eternal separation is exactly why salvation is man's greatest need! Thankfully, however, God provided Jesus for the salvation of all who believe in Him.

The Basis of Salvation

God's ultimate desire is to be in fellowship with humans. He was in fellowship with Adam until Adam sinned, and from that point on, humanity's sinfulness has separated us from God. Though humans were separated from God, it never diminished God's love for us nor His longing to be in fellowship with all humans. So, God developed a plan. He knew that humans would sin before He created them, and He had a plan of redemption in place before the world was created. "You were not redeemed with corruptible things, like silver or gold, from your aimless conduct received by tradition from your fathers, but with the precious blood of Christ, as of a lamb without blemish and without spot. He indeed was foreordained before the foundation of the world, but was manifest in these last times for you" (1 Peter 1:18–20 NKJV).

God had already provided the answer to the problem of sin before the first sin happened—that's how much He loves us! His answer is simple: "For God so loved the world, that he gave his only Son, that whoever believes in him should not perish but have eternal life" (John 3:16 ESV).

The dilemma caused by the collision of God's holiness with our sinfulness was solved by the atonement. The atonement of Jesus Christ is just another way of saying Christ bore the penalty for our sins. God's holiness was satisfied when Jesus, the sinless sacrifice, accepted the penalty of sin on the cross. God's justice required a sacrifice for sin, and Jesus became that sacrifice. When God raised Jesus from the grave, He became "the firstborn from among the dead, so that in everything he might have the supremacy" (Colossians 1:18). Jesus is firstborn in that those who believe in Him will also rise from the dead because our sins have been forgiven. Look at the following verses:

- For God so loved the world that he gave his one and only Son, that whoever believes in him shall not perish but have eternal life. For God did not send his Son into the world to condemn the world, but to save the world through him. (John 3:16–17)

- "For even the Son of Man did not come to be served, but to serve, and to give his life as a ransom for many." (Mark 10:45)

- But God demonstrates his own love for us in this: While we were still sinners, Christ died for us. (Romans 5:8)

- For what I received I passed on to you as of first importance: that Christ died for our sins according to the Scriptures, that he was buried, that he was raised on the third day according to the Scriptures. (1 Corinthians 15:3–4)

- "He himself bore our sins" in his body on the cross, so that we might die to sins and live for righteousness; "by his wounds you have been healed." (1 Peter 2:24)

Jesus sacrificed Himself so that we may become holy, righteous, and accepted by God just as He is. That's worth praising God for!

Through all of this wonderful news, there is one word that makes all of it possible: *grace.* Peter said that God is the God of all grace (1 Peter 5:10). A simple definition of grace is this: "God deals favorably with people in a way they do not deserve."[1] The problem that sin causes and the solution that God offers through the perfect atonement of Jesus is all brought about by God's grace. "For by grace you have been saved through faith, and that not of yourselves; it is the gift of God, not of works, lest anyone should boast" (Ephesians 2:8–9 NKJV). Overall, we have much to thank God for, because through His grace He sent Jesus to the cross to bear our punishment so that we may be saved! Let us rejoice with John in saying, "Behold what manner of love the Father has bestowed on us, that we should be called children of God!" (1 John 3:1 NKJV). And we are!

How to Be Saved

All of this wonderful news leads us to the most important question we will ever answer: How then, shall I be saved? Through God's grace, salvation is a gift—the greatest gift ever given to humanity—and therefore it must be received. Thankfully, the Bible is very clear on how to receive this wonderful gift! There are two key words that will be discussed in this chapter to explain how to be saved. The first is *faith.* Faith is the means by which we are saved. In Ephesians 2:8–9, Paul says that we have been saved by grace through faith.

Though we are saved *by* grace, we are saved *through* faith. Look at it this way: grace is God's part in salvation, and faith is our part in salvation. Putting faith in Jesus Christ means that we place our trust in Jesus as our Savior. Jesus Himself said, "Therefore I said to you that you will die in your sins; for unless you believe that I am He, you will die in your sins" (John 8:24 NASB). A person must believe that Jesus is who He says He is, the one who can save the world. Romans 10:9–10 gives one of the clearest examples in the New Testament on how to be saved: "If you declare with your mouth, 'Jesus is Lord,' and believe in your heart that God raised him from the dead, you will be saved. For it is with your heart that you believe and are justified, and it is with your mouth that you profess your faith and are saved." Believing in Jesus through faith is the first step toward receiving salvation.

The second key word is *repentance*. Faith coupled with repentance results in salvation. Repentance literally means "to change your mind." So, repenting of your sin to be saved means you must "change your mind" about your sin to be saved. This kind of repentance simply means that you acknowledge that your sin is an affront to God and separates you from Him. While you are under conviction (the Holy Spirit drawing you to God), you realize that your sin is wrong and ask Jesus to forgive you as you turn from your sin and turn to God. Repentance from sin means your mind changes to a state where you agree it was sin that separated you from God. Paul summarized his ministry in Acts 20:20–21. "I have not hesitated to preach anything that would be helpful to you but have taught you publicly and from house to house. I have declared to both Jews and Greeks that they must turn to

God in repentance and have faith in our Lord Jesus." Paul declared that the central focus of his teaching is turning from sin toward God and having faith in Jesus. In other words, Paul said that salvation lies in changing your mind, or choosing to love God more than sin, and placing your faith in the work and person of Jesus Christ. When a person does those two things sincerely, he or she will receive the gift of salvation.

Life Answers

Salvation is a popular word that is many times taken for granted. Pastors and teachers often believe that the majority of the people who hear their preaching or teaching understand what salvation means and how they can be saved. Unfortunately, this is not always the case. Hopefully, after reading this chapter, you have a much better understanding of what salvation is, how it applies to you, and how you can share this great truth with nonbelievers.

Points to Remember

1. Salvation means different things, but the most important meaning is to rescue from sin.

2. God is holy, and man is sinful, creating a great dilemma for humanity and God.

3. God, in love, sent Jesus to pay the ultimate price to atone for the sins of humanity.

4. Salvation is by God's grace alone.

5. A person who sincerely repents of sin and places his or her faith in Jesus will be saved.

Notes

1 Floyd H. Barackman, *Practical Christian Theology*, 4th ed. (Grand Rapids, MI: Kregel, 2001), 342.

Chapter 8

Who Is the Holy Spirit?

The Facts about the Third Person of the Trinity

"But the Advocate, the Holy Spirit, whom the Father will send in my name, will teach you all things and will remind you of everything I have said to you." — John 14:26

Francis Chan wrote a great book about the Holy Spirit called *Forgotten God.*[1] Chan titled the book as he did because he felt the Holy Spirit has been neglected, often ignored, and nearly forgotten in daily life. I believe he has a valid point. While no Christian who believes the Bible would deny the existence of the Holy Spirit, and most would recognize the Holy Spirit as the third person of the Trinity, there is often a lack of knowledge in many Christians' minds regarding the Holy Spirit. Many Christians cannot tell you about His function in the believer's life, nor do they experience the presence of the Holy Spirit in the manner of the first-century believer. This chapter provides an introduction to the identity and role of the Holy Spirit.

The Holy Spirit's Identity

The first thing to understand about the Holy Spirit is that He is not an "it," an apparition, or something resembling "the Force" from a Star Wars movie. The Holy Spirit is the living third person of the Trinity. The Bible teaches that the Holy Spirit is God,[2] and God is a person, so therefore the Holy Spirit must be a person as well. We find in Scripture the Holy Spirit is often referenced by pronouns. For example, Acts 13:2 reads, "While they were worshiping the Lord and fasting, the Holy Spirit said, 'Set apart for me Barnabas and Saul for the work to which I have called them.'" In this instance Luke, writing under the influence and by the power of the Holy Spirit, records the Holy Spirit referring to Himself as "I."

The Holy Spirit also possesses certain elements of personality. We know the Holy Spirit possesses intellect, and therefore has a mind, because Romans 8:27 says: "And he who searches our hearts knows the mind of the Spirit, because the Spirit intercedes for God's people in accordance with the will of God." In addition, the Holy Spirit possesses wisdom, something a simple "force" or "influence" cannot possess. Isaiah 11:2 says,

> The Spirit of the LORD will rest on him—
> the Spirit of wisdom and of understanding.

We know the Holy Spirit possesses emotions, since Romans 15:30 establishes the Holy Spirit is capable of loving: "I urge you, brothers and sisters, by our Lord Jesus Christ and by the love of the Spirit, to join me in my struggle by praying to God for me." Also, Paul makes it clear in Ephesians the Holy Spirit can be grieved: "And do not grieve the Holy Spirit of God, with whom you were sealed for the day of redemption" (4:30).

Finally, the Holy Spirit possesses a will. As we saw earlier, Acts 13:2 records the Spirit instructing Paul and Barnabas based on the Spirit's will. "While they were worshiping the Lord and fasting, the Holy Spirit said, 'Set apart for me Barnabas and Saul for the work to which I have called them.'" So we can conclude the Holy Spirit, possessing all of the characteristics of individuality, is the living third person of the Trinity.

The Holy Spirit in the Trinity

The Holy Spirit's deity is well established throughout the Bible. We have established the Holy Spirit is a person, so now we will turn our attention to establishing the case the Holy Spirit is God. We know this first because the Holy Spirit shares many attributes of God. Below is a list of these attributes along with the verses that state this truth.

- *The Holy Spirit is eternal.* "How much more will the blood of Christ, who through the eternal Spirit offered himself without blemish to God, purify our conscience from dead works to serve the living God" (Hebrews 9:14 ESV).

- *The Holy Spirit possesses life within Himself, as He is called the Spirit of Life.* "For the law of the Spirit of life has set you free in Christ Jesus from the law of sin and death" (Romans 8:2 ESV).

- *The Holy Spirit is omnipresent, or present everywhere at any time.*

> Where shall I go from your Spirit?
> Or where shall I flee from your presence?

If I ascend to heaven, you are there!
If I make my bed in Sheol, you are there!
If I take the wings of the morning
    and dwell in the uttermost parts of the sea,
even there your hand shall lead me,
    and your right hand shall hold me. (Psalm
        139:7–10 ESV)

- *The Holy Spirit is omniscient.* "For the Spirit searches everything, even the depths of God. For who knows a person's thoughts except the spirit of that person, which is in him? So also no one comprehends the thoughts of God except the Spirit of God" (1 Corinthians 2:10–11 ESV).

- *The Holy Spirit has divine foreknowledge.* "Brothers, the Scripture had to be fulfilled, which the Holy Spirit spoke beforehand by the mouth of David concerning Judas, who became a guide to those who arrested Jesus" (Acts 1:16 ESV).

These are just a few of the attributes that the Holy Spirit shares with God, giving evidence of the Holy Spirit's function in the Trinity.

Another way that the Holy Spirit functions in the Trinity is that the Holy Spirit was actively involved in creation. Genesis 1:1–2 reads, "In the beginning God created the heavens and the earth. Now the earth was formless and empty, darkness was over the surface of the deep, and the Spirit of God was hovering over the waters." Job also notes that the Spirit helped create humankind. "The Spirit of God has made me; / the breath of the Almighty gives me life" (Job 33:4). In both of these instances, the Spirit is shown to take part in what God is credited with doing, creating both the universe and humans. Thus, the Spirit functions as a Creator with the other two members of the Trinity.

The Holy Spirit's Function in the Believer's Life

One of the greatest promises Jesus gave believers is the coming of the Holy Spirit into the lives of all who believe. He told the disciples, "But the Helper, the Holy Spirit, whom the Father will send in My name, He will teach you all things, and bring to your remembrance all that I said to you" (John 14:26 NASB). This gift of the Holy Spirit was rare and specifically placed in the Old Testament but is now promised to anyone who believes upon the Lord Jesus Christ. Sadly, the Holy Spirit's function in the life of many believers is largely unknown. Many believers are unaware of how the Holy Spirit works in our lives. Let's explore some of the ways the Holy Spirit manifests Himself in the life of a believer.

The Holy Spirit guides people into truth. Just as the children of Israel were led by a pillar of fire at night and a cloud of smoke by day, God the Spirit guides us in our journey through life! Jesus told His disciples, "When the Spirit of truth comes, he will guide you into all the truth, for he will not speak on his own authority" (John 16:13 ESV). The Bible doesn't answer every explicit, direct question we encounter in life. God's Word reveals godly principles to lead us into wisdom and into a closer relationship with Him through Christ by the power of the Holy Spirit. For those questions the Bible does not explicitly answer, the Holy Spirit will guide us into the truth of God!

The Holy Spirit teaches us God's deep truths in a way we can understand. First Corinthians 2:13 says, "This is what we speak, not in words taught us by human wisdom but in words taught by the Spirit, explaining spiritual realities with Spirit-taught words." Jesus also told His disciples that the Holy Spirit would teach them all things and remind them of everything that Jesus had taught them (John 14:26). In this sense, the Holy Spirit teaches people as they navigate through life. Those who take the time to pray and listen to the Holy Spirit can learn lessons many different ways through Him.

The Holy Spirit brings conviction, helping people to discern the difference between right and wrong. Jesus told the disciples, "And He, when He comes, will convict the world concerning sin and righteousness and judgment" (John 16:8 NASB). This is one of the greatest and most overlooked works of the Holy Spirit. Sometimes the conviction of the Holy Spirit guides people away from sin. At other times He will convict people after they have sinned, so that if they respond with repentance they can experience the blessing of God's forgiveness.

The Holy Spirit speaks to people. When the Holy Spirit speaks to us, God is speaking to us. Paul wrote in Galatians 4:6, "Because you are his sons, God sent the Spirit of his Son into our hearts, the Spirit who calls out, 'Abba, Father.'" Paul also wrote later in the New Testament, "Now the Spirit expressly says that in later times some will depart from the faith by devoting themselves to deceitful spirits and teachings of demons" (1 Timothy 4:1 ESV). Both of these instances demonstrate the Holy Spirit speaking to Christians. Though God may not speak to us audibly, He has given the Holy Spirit to speak to Christians in a unique way.

The Holy Spirit intercedes for believers. Read this remarkable passage in Romans 8: "Likewise the Spirit also helps in our weaknesses. For we do not know what we should pray for as we ought, but the Spirit Himself makes intercession for us with groanings which cannot be uttered. Now He who searches the hearts knows what the mind of the Spirit is, because He makes intercession for the saints according to the will of God" (verses 26–27 NKJV). Even when we are not sure what to pray, or we feel like we just can't pray, the Holy Spirit understands us much better than we understand ourselves, and He intercedes on our behalf to God the Father.

The Holy Spirit distributes spiritual gifts to the church.

> For to one is given through the Spirit the utterance of wisdom, and to another the utterance of knowledge according to the same Spirit, to another faith by the same Spirit, to another gifts of healing by the one Spirit, to another the working of miracles, to another prophecy, to another the ability to distinguish between spirits, to another various kinds of tongues, to another the interpretation of tongues. All these are empowered by one and the same Spirit, who apportions to each one individually as he wills. (1 Corinthians 12:8–11 ESV)

According to this passage, the Holy Spirit chooses the spiritual gifts each person will receive; and in His infinite wisdom, He empowers us to work together, combining our gifts with the gifts of others to accomplish His divine purpose.

Just as the Holy Spirit distributes gifts, He appoints leaders in the church. In Acts 20:28, Paul says, "Keep watch over yourselves and all the flock of which the Holy Spirit has made you overseers. Be shepherds of the church of God, which he bought with his own blood." Paul acknowledged that the Holy Spirit had made the Ephesian elders overseers. In the same sense, we should trust the Holy Spirit to help guide our churches in choosing leaders.

The Holy Spirit is also to be obeyed. To disobey a prodding of the Holy Spirit is to disobey God. However, obedience to the Holy Spirit often results in great reward. For example, when Philip was in the middle of a revival among the Samaritans, the Holy Spirit commanded him to leave a fruitful ministry and go to a seemingly fruitless place to speak to an Ethiopian official. Philip, without understanding, did as he was told and had the opportunity to explain the gospel to a man who would take the gospel message back to Ethiopia (Acts 8:30–39). In Acts 10:9–16 we are told that God gave Peter a vision of a sheet coming down from heaven, filled with all kinds of unclean animals. God commanded Peter to "kill and eat" even though every fiber of Peter's Jewish being cried out in protest. But he obeyed God, and the Holy Spirit gave him the opportunity to explain the gospel to a Roman centurion named Cornelius (Acts 10:17–48).

While obedience to the Holy Spirit brings blessing and life, deceiving the Holy Spirit can bring death. In Acts 5:1–11, Luke tells the tragic story of Ananias and Sapphira, who sold a piece of property and led everyone to believe they gave all of the proceeds to the church while instead holding back some of the proceeds for themselves. Peter confronted

Ananias asking, "How is it that Satan has so filled your heart that you have lied to the Holy Spirit and have kept for yourself some of the money you received for the land?" (verse 3). Upon hearing those words Ananias dropped dead on the spot! Later, Sapphira came, and before Peter she supported her husband's lie and suffered his fate. The result was that "great fear seized the whole church and all who heard about these events" (verse 11).

Life Answers

The role and work of the Holy Spirit is perhaps the best kept secret within Christianity. Believers should know about and embrace the Holy Spirit's work and role so that we may experience the blessings that accompany His presence in our lives. As a member of the Trinity, the Holy Spirit functions as God in an incredibly personal way to the believer. I hope after reading this you will recognize the untapped resource that is living within every believer—the Holy Spirit!

Points to Remember

1. The Holy Spirit is a person, not a force or influence.
2. The Holy Spirit is the third person of the Trinity, sharing many attributes with God.
3. The Holy Spirit has many functions in the believer's life.

Notes

[1] Francis Chan, *Forgotten God* (Colorado Springs: David C. Cook, 2009).

[2] See Acts 5:3–4, or see "God the Spirit" in chapter 9.

Chapter 9

What Is the Trinity?

How Can God Be Three Persons in One Being?

May the grace of the Lord Jesus Christ, and the love of God, and the fellowship of the Holy Spirit be with you all. — 2 Corinthians 13:14

The Bible contains many mysteries. We should not fear or be stressed about a mystery, because an exhaustive knowledge of God is beyond our capacity as finite beings. A *mystery* is simply the full meaning of God's attributes or actions that are hidden from us in the present but will ultimately be revealed in the future. Thankfully, the coming of Christ and His fulfillment of the law cleared up some of the mysteries in the Old Testament. Additionally, all the mysterious prophecies in the Old Testament regarding the Messiah were fulfilled through Jesus's miraculous birth, sinless life, and glorious resurrection. Yet, some mysteries still exist, and many will remain a mystery until we come face-to-face with the Lord Jesus Christ in heaven. Perhaps the grandest and most misunderstood mystery of all is the Godhead, commonly referred to as the Trinity.

The Trinity has been a source of debate among Christians since the fourth century. Very early (first-century) references to the relationship between the Father, the Son, and the Holy Spirit, were expressed in baptismal formulas. Converts would be baptized three times, once in the name of the Father, then in the name of the Son, and, finally, in the name of the Holy Spirit. This was not full-blown Trinitarian theology, but it did represent an early understanding of God as both one and three. The most significant attack against this early understanding of God's nature came from Arius, who was "a senior presbyter in charge of Baucalis, one of the twelve 'parishes' of Alexandria."[1] His insistence that the Father alone was really God and that the Son was of a similar, yet different, essence than the Father was vigorously rejected by Bishop Alexander. Arius, his followers, and his theology were rejected at the Council of Nicaea in AD 324. The Nicene Creed affirmed the unity of the Father, Son, and the Holy Spirit, and should have put an end to any controversy over the idea of the Trinity. However, the conflict would rage on until the Council of Chalcedon in 451 put an end to Arianism within the Roman Empire. Modern-day detractors who identify as Christian and strongly question Trinitarian theology include Oneness Pentecostals, such as The Church of God International and the United Church of God. Some of the philosophies that push back against Trinitarianism include Adoptionism (Jesus is adopted by the Father), Modalism (the Father, Son, and Holy Spirit exist as three separate entities), and Subordinationism (the Son is subordinate to the Father, and the Holy Spirit is subordinate to the Son and the Father).

Muslims and Jews often accuse Christians of serving three different gods rather than one because they misunderstand the Trinity. Many atheists add that the Trinity is an apparent contradiction to Christianity's claim to monotheism, or the belief in one God. While it is true the vast majority of Christians accept the doctrine of the Trinity, few can explain or defend the doctrine using Scripture. This chapter is to help identify why each member of the Trinity is God, and how, though three persons, the Trinity is one God.

Monotheism in the Bible

Monotheism, or the belief that there is one God, is the core belief of Christianity. Both Judaism and Islam affirm a monotheistic understanding of the nature of God. Almost every Christian would agree there is only one true God; the God known as *Yahweh*, *Jehovah*, and *Adonai* who reveals Himself in the Old Testament. This is the same God who created the heavens and the earth; the sea and all that is in it; and all plants, animals, organisms, and people. This is the same God who chose Abraham and his descendants to become the nation of Israel. God developed a unique relationship with Israel, setting them apart as His chosen people, and drawing the ancient world to Himself through that relationship.

From the very beginning, the God of Israel revealed Himself as one God. There could be no belief in any other gods. Central to Israel's unique covenant with God was Israel's essential creed was that God is one. Deuteronomy 6 reads,

> "Hear, O Israel: The LORD our God, the LORD is one! You shall love the LORD your God with all your heart, with all your soul, and with all your strength.
>
> And these words which I command you today shall be in your heart. You shall teach them diligently to your children . . . You shall bind them as a sign on your hand, and they shall be as frontlets between your eyes. You shall

write them on the doorposts of your house and on your gates." (verses 4–9 NKJV)

The first verse of the passage is known as the *Shema*, and every believing Jewish family would teach this verse to their children. Many Jewish men would put these words written on parchment in small leather boxes (called *phylacteries*) and strap one to their forehead or around their left arm. They also placed a small case (called a *mezuzah*) on the doorpost of their houses as a reminder of their belief in the one God of Israel.

In Exodus 20:1–17, we read that Moses gave the Ten Commandments to Israel. The first commandment is to have no other gods before Yahweh. This commandment was given first to remind all of creation there is only one God, and He is the God of Abraham, Isaac, and Jacob.

The Old Testament contains stories of epic battles between the one true God of Israel and the gods of wood and stone made by human hands. Stories such as the one recorded in 1 Kings 18:20–40, where Elijah, the great prophet of God, confronts and totally defeats the false prophets of Baal, dramatically illustrate the truth that there is only one God and *Yahweh* is His name!

This monotheistic understanding of God carries over into the New Testament. Jesus quotes the Shema in Mark 12:29, affirming the monotheistic nature of God (and of Himself as part of the Trinity). Paul declares, "There is one God" in 1 Timothy 2:5; and he affirms that every other god is a false god in 1 Corinthians 8:4: "So then, about eating food sacrificed to idols: We know that 'An idol is nothing at all in the world' and that 'There is no God but one.'" For a more complete understanding of this important doctrine, let's take a look at the members of the Trinity.

God the Father

God is rarely referred to as *Father* in the Old Testament. Psalm 68:5 calls God a "father to the fatherless." In Psalm 89:26, the psalmist refers to God as his Father. God is referred to as the Father of the nation of Israel in Deuteronomy 32:6 and in Isaiah 63:16 and 64:8. He is referred to fifteen times as the Father of certain individuals, and the imagery of God as Father (without the name) can be found nine times from Exodus to Malachi.

The understanding of "God the Father" came to fruition when "God the Son" came to earth and demonstrated the distinction between Himself and His Father. Simon Chan, writing for *Christianity Today* said, "In the New Testament, God's fatherhood conveys two distinct ideas. First, it refers primarily to the internal relationship within the Trinity. Second, the Father metaphor points to God as the Creator (Isa. 64:8; Mal. 2:10).[2]

Jesus referred to God as His Father many times. The Sermon on the Mount, found in Matthew 5–7, references the idea of calling God "Father." In these chapters Jesus mentions giving glory to the Father in heaven (5:16); people being children of the Father (5:45); being perfect as the heavenly Father is perfect (5:48); giving in secret so the Father who sees in secret will give a reward (6:1–4); praying to the Father in heaven (6:5–14); receiving good gifts from the Father (7:11), and other mentions of the Father in those chapters. Earlier in Matthew's Gospel, God the Father spoke from heaven affirming Jesus as His Son, "This is My beloved Son, in whom I am well pleased" (3:17 NKJV). Jesus, perhaps to help the people understand the distinctions between the persons of the Trinity, brought into practice the naming of God as Father. Paul picked this up in his epistles, often referring to God as Father (see Romans 1:7; 6:4; 15:6; 1 Corinthians 1:3; 2 Corinthians 1:2; Galatians 1:1; Ephesians 1:2).

God the Son

With all of this scriptural evidence, it should be easy to believe that God the Father is God. The Bible also speaks clearly about the Son being God. For example, John 5:18 reads, "For this reason [the Jews] tried all the more to kill him; not only was he breaking the Sabbath, but he was even calling God his own Father, making himself equal with God." Later, John's Gospel records that Jesus said, "I and the Father are one" (10:30). A few verses later, John wrote, "'We are not stoning you for any good work,' [the Jews] replied, 'but for blasphemy, because you, a mere man, claim to be God'" (verse 33). Responding to a request from Philip that He "show us the Father," Jesus said, "Don't you know me, Philip, even after I been among you such a long time? Anyone who has seen me has seen the Father. How can you say, 'Show us the Father'?" (14:8–9).

How can God and Jesus be one if Jesus is not God? Clearly, the Jews believed that Jesus's claims were ascribing deity to Himself. John also wrote specifically that Christ is God in

John 1:1 and 1:14 when he equated the Word as God (verse 1) and then said, "And the Word became flesh, and dwelt among us, and we saw His glory, glory as of the only begotten from the Father, full of grace and truth" (verse 14 NASB).

Jesus also claimed to possess equal glory with God the Father before the world began in John 17:5: "And now, Father, glorify me in your presence with the glory I had with you before the world began."

Jesus said that He was to be honored in the same way people honored the Father: "The Father judges no one, but has given all judgment to the Son, that all may honor the Son, just as they honor the Father. Whoever does not honor the Son does not honor the Father who sent him" (John 5:22–23 ESV).

Jesus revealed His ability to meet anyone's spiritual needs. He told the woman at the well in John 4:14, "Whoever drinks the water I give them will never thirst. Indeed, the water I give them will become in them a spring of water welling up to eternal life." He also said to a crowd in John 6:35, "I am the bread of life. Whoever comes to me will never go hungry, and whoever believes in me will never be thirsty."

Finally, Jesus claimed to give everlasting life to anyone who trusts in Him. He told Nicodemus, "For God so loved the world that He gave His only begotten Son, that whoever believes in Him should not perish but have everlasting life" (John 3:16 NKJV). In John 11:26 Jesus adds, "Whoever lives and believes in Me shall never die. Do you believe this?"

From all of this evidence, Christ should be understood as God because of His remarkable claims, the Jews' perception of Him, and His ability to meet people's spiritual needs in the same way God would meet them.

God the Spirit

As we said in the last chapter, the Holy Spirit is the lesser understood of the persons in the Trinity, or as Francis Chan has said, the "forgotten God."[3] Yet it is important to know about the Holy Spirit if He is indeed God. Consider these verses from Acts 5: "But Peter said, 'Ananias, why has Satan filled your heart to lie to the Holy Spirit and keep back part of the price of the land for yourself? . . . You have not lied to men but to God'" (verses 3–4 NKJV). These verse demonstrate how Peter equated the Holy Spirit with God, as he told Ananias that by lying to one, he had lied to the other.

Paul also makes a similar statement ascribing the equality of the Spirit with God. In 1 Corinthians 3:16 Paul wrote, "Don't you know that you yourselves are God's temple and that God's Spirit dwells in your midst?" A few chapters later in 1 Corinthians 6:19, Paul says, "Do you not know that your bodies are temples of the Holy Spirit, who is in you, whom you have received from God? You are not your own." Just as Paul said people are temples of God, he also said people are temples of the Holy Spirit, equating the Holy Spirit with God.

The Community of the Trinity

Thus far, this chapter has explained how God is one, yet also how the Father, the Son, and the Holy Spirit meet the qualifications of God. This seems to create a puzzle, as three different persons meet the qualification of God, yet there can only be one. This is the divine mystery of the Trinity. Though there are three separate beings, they exist as one.

The fact that God is infinitely complex and far beyond what our minds could ever comprehend helps us accept by faith the mystery of the Trinity. However, there are some naturally occurring analogies that while painting an incomplete picture may help get us closer to a proper understanding.

One such analogy compares the Trinity to water. Water, or H_2O, can exist in three different states: solid, liquid, and gas. When the temperature of water drops below 32 degrees Fahrenheit, the result is a solid substance called *ice*. When the temperature of water is raised above 212 degrees Fahrenheit, the result is a gas called *steam*. In its natural state, water is a liquid. Whether the water is ice, water, or steam, it never changes its identity from H_2O. The only thing this analogy fails to capture, when compared to the Trinity, is that water can exist only as liquid, solid, or gas—one of the three—at a given time. It cannot exist in all three states at the same time. The members of the Trinity, though never losing their identity of God, exist simultaneously at all times.

Life Answers

The Trinity is one of the hardest theological realities in the Bible to grasp. We will not fully comprehend the mystery of the Trinity while we exist in this fleshly and sinful body. Yet, one day, when we enter eternity with Christ, we will understand all things. Paul stated this clearly: "For now we see in a mirror dimly, but then face to face; now I know in part, but then I will know fully just as I also have been fully known" (1 Corinthians 13:12 NASB). The important thing to understand from this chapter is even though the vast majority of

Christians believe in a triune God, it does not mean that Christians believe in three separate Gods. The Bible presents one God who exists as one, in three separate expressions.

Points to Remember

1. The Bible teaches only monotheism in both the Old and New Testaments.

2. The Bible provides sufficient evidence that the Father is God.

3. The Bible provides sufficient evidence that the Son is God.

4. The Bible provides sufficient evidence that the Spirit is God.

5. The Trinity is impossible to comprehend, but its truth is nevertheless found within Scripture and can be believed without compromising God's command of monotheism.

Notes

[1] Tim Dowley, ed., *Introduction to the History of Christianity*, 2nd ed. (Minneapolis: Fortress Press, 2013), 118.

[2] Simon Chan, "Why We Call God 'Father,'" *Christianity Today,* July/August 2013, 48, http://www.christianitytoday.com/ct/2013/july-august/why-we-call-god-father.html.

[3] Francis Chan, *Forgotten God* (Colorado Springs: David C. Cook, 2009).

Chapter 10

What Happens When We Die?

Answers from Scripture about Heaven, Hell, and the Afterlife

"Then they will go away to eternal punishment, but the righteous to eternal life." — Matthew 25:46

Woody Allen once said, "It's not that I am afraid to die, I just don't want to be there when it happens."[1] Allen surely said this in jest; but in reality, it captures the typical reaction to death. The vast majority of people realize the inevitability of death and taxes, but most are reluctant or even reticent to face this final reality. In other words, everybody's talking about heaven, but nobody wants to die. I remember an old preacher's joke where a pastor is thundering away in the pulpit about heaven and hell, and at some point, he asks, "How many of you want to go to heaven?" Everyone in the congregation raised their hands except this one older gentleman in the back. The preacher challenged the man, asking indignantly, "Sir, don't you want to go to heaven when you die?" The old man answered, "Oh sure, preacher, I want to go to heaven when I die, but it sounded to me you were trying to get up a load to go tonight!"

Funerals often make people uncomfortable because they bring people face-to-face with the fact of their own mortality. The life of a loved one is celebrated, yet those left behind are grief-stricken as they realize all the things their loved one did, and their every essence ended with the person's life. All that remains is the memory of the loved one's life and legacy and the pain of separation. Many times funeral goers are left to ponder their own life and legacy, and the dreaded "what if" questions begin to surface. Typically the older a person gets, both the frequency and intensity of the "what if" questions grows stronger. *What if I die tomorrow? What if my legacy is lost because people forget I ever lived? What if my family falters because I have left them behind?* All of these "what if" questions are extremely important, but the most important question we can ask is, *what really happens when I die?* If we answer this question correctly, the "what if" questions will take care of themselves.

Questions about the afterlife have captivated the minds of humanity throughout history. Every culture deals with death differently, leading to the development of multiple burial rituals that rise from the cultural understanding of the afterlife. The Egyptians would often bury their dead in tombs with their personal belongings, believing the belongings will accompany the person to the afterlife. The Egyptians believed the soul could not exist without the body, so preservation of the body was essential to their burial customs. Hindus usually burn the deceased and scatter the person's ashes in a river. Their worldview teaches that just as a river carries the ashes into the ocean, so does the soul flow into Brahman to be kept or recycled in a new life. Ancient Greeks and Romans constructed monuments to ensure a proper send-off into the afterlife. The modern-day practice of erecting tombstones over gravesites is a distant echo of that tradition. In parts of China, the people believe the dead live on as spirits capable of interfering with the world of the living, so they developed the practice of ancestor worship. Ultimately, all cultures realize their own mortality and respond by establishing elaborate burial rituals for their dead.

God's Word reveals the truth about death and the afterlife. Though many of the details are not revealed and would likely go beyond the comprehension of the human mind, God, in His mercy and love for us, has provided enough detail in the Bible to help us understand much of what the afterlife will be like. This chapter will focus on what heaven is like, what hell is like, and how a Christian should respond to death.

Heaven in the Bible

The Bible describes two places in the afterlife that are commonly referred to as *heaven* and *hell*. Before we look at what the Bible says about heaven, it is important to understand there are different meanings of the word, based on the usage and context of the passage. For example, Genesis 1:1 speaks of "the heavens" in regard to the universe outside the earth: "In the beginning God created the heavens and the earth." The heavens in this verse are the actual skies, the stars, planets, and galaxies—in short, the universe. Other verses in the Bible refer to this kind of heaven as well: "The heavens are telling of the glory of God; / And their expanse is declaring the work of His hands" (Psalm 19:1 NASB).[2] This heaven is simply the natural creation of God.

The Bible also uses the heavens to refer to the dwelling place of God. Psalm 115:3 in the New American Standard Bible proclaims, "Our God is in the heavens; / He does whatever He pleases." Jesus referred often to the Father as being in heaven: "In the same way, let your light shine before others, so that they may see your good works and give glory to your Father who is in heaven" (Matthew 5:16 ESV).[3] Jesus is said to come from heaven, referring to the dwelling place of God: "For I have come down from heaven, not to do my own will but the will of him who sent me" (John 6:38 ESV). Paul also supports Jesus's statement in 1 Corinthians 15: "The first man [Adam] was of the dust of the earth; the second man [Jesus] is of heaven" (verse 47). The place where the Godhead dwells, which is a mystery to man, is referred to as *heaven*.

Heaven for a born-again believer is often portrayed as a beautiful and immense gated city where inhabitants float on their own personal cloud while listening to harp music. Although this vision of heaven has its own appeal, it is a far cry from what the Bible reveals heaven is like.

No one knows for sure exactly what heaven is like, but the Bible does give us some clues. We know that it is a place so incredibly beautiful it is beyond the scope of our imagination. Paul wrote in 1 Corinthians 2:

> But as it is written:
> "Eye has seen, nor ear heard,
> Nor have entered into the heart of man
> The things which God has prepared for those
>   who love Him." (verse 9 NKJV)

Living in our world blurs our vision of heaven because this world is dominated by sin and the effects of the fall. Heaven will be totally void of anything that does not align with God's will. It will be perfect, and therefore perfectly suited for those of us who have been made perfect by His blood.

The second thing of which we can be assured that all believers will be there! Paul wrote that he was "well pleased rather to be absent from the body and to be present with the Lord" (2 Corinthians 5:8 NKJV). This verse gives hope that when a believer dies he or she goes immediately to be with the Lord. Some people believe that Christians will be in some sort of spiritual sleep until Christ returns, but the Bible clearly teaches that we will go to be with God immediately upon death. However, most scholars do believe that this is an intermediary state, meaning that Christians will only be in this "heaven" until God creates a new heaven and earth.

The Bible teaches it is the soul that goes to be with God upon death, while the body is left behind on earth. However, when Christ returns, the bodies of the saints will be resurrected. Paul describes this victorious process in 1 Corinthians 15.

> Behold, I tell you a mystery: We shall not all sleep, but we shall all be changed—in a moment, in the twinkling of an eye, at the last trumpet. For the trumpet will sound, and the dead will be raised incorruptible, and we shall be changed. For this corruptible must put on incorruption, and this mortal must put on immortality. So when this corruptible has put on incorruption, and this mortal has put on immortality, then shall be brought to pass the saying that is written: "Death is swallowed up in victory."

"O Death, where is your sting?
O Hades, where is your victory?"

The sting of death is sin, and the strength of sin is
the law. But thanks be to God, who gives us the victory
through our Lord Jesus Christ. (verses 51–57 NKJV)

God will resurrect the bodies of all believers, transforming them into a glorified, perfect body similar to the resurrected body of Jesus. We know Jesus's resurrected body
retained His physical appearance because He was recognized
by His disciples. But it also took on supernatural characteristics, such as the ability to pass through solid structures.
John 20 records, "So when it was evening on that day, the
first day of the week, and when the doors were shut where
the disciples were, for fear of the Jews, Jesus came and stood
in their midst and said to them, 'Peace be with you'" (verse
19 NASB). Thomas was not present on this occasion, and
until a few days later, he doubted the account given to him
by the other disciples. Again John records, "After eight days
His disciples were again inside, and Thomas with them. Jesus came, the doors having been shut, and stood in their
midst and said, 'Peace be with you'" (verse 26 NASB). Both
of these appearances of Jesus emphasize the fact the doors
were locked, and Jesus simply appeared, meaning His resurrected body was not subject to this world's physical laws.

Luke's Gospel records the encounter Jesus had with the
two disciples on the road to Emmaus. Again, we see evidence
that Jesus's resurrected body, although physical in nature,
was not bound by time and space. Jesus had been walking
along the road with the two disciples, and when they reached

their village, Jesus indicated He intended to keep going. But the two disciples persuaded Him to stay for the evening meal. Here, Luke picks up the story saying, "When He had reclined at the table with them, He took the bread and blessed it, and breaking it, He began giving it to them. Then their eyes were opened and they recognized Him; and He vanished from their sight" (24:30–31 NASB). All during the journey to Emmaus, Jesus concealed His identity from them, and when they recognized Him, He supernaturally disappeared from their presence. While we don't know exactly what our resurrected bodies will be like, these stories about Jesus's post-resurrection appearances give us a glimpse of what is in store for us when our souls and our new glorified bodies are united.

During this time, God will also establish a new physical heaven and a new physical earth for the resurrected bodies to inhabit eternally. John wrote in Revelation 21:1, "Then I saw 'a new heaven and a new earth,' for the first heaven and the first earth had passed away, and there was no longer any sea." The new heaven and earth will be filled with the presence and glory of God, returning to a state similar to the original creation before the effects of the fall. This is where Christians will live eternally in complete joy and bliss! This is the eternal dwelling place of God's people.

Hell in the Bible

The beauty, blessings, and glory of heaven stand in stark contrast to the horror of hell. Although not a popular topic for the pulpit, the classroom, or the Sunday school class, hell is a real place with real suffering that never eases up or goes away. Mark described the everlasting nature of hell as a place, "where '[the] worm does not die / And the fire is not quenched'" (Mark 9:48 NKJV).

When an unsaved person dies, you rarely hear anyone refer to the fact they are now separated from God forever in hell. I have never been to a funeral where the officiant suggested the deceased person was in hell. Even if the officiant believes that to be true, based on the deceased's rejection of Jesus Christ as Savior, he or she would most likely avoid the topic because the subject brings up such strong emotions. No one wants to believe their loved one is lost forever, and yet that is exactly what the Bible teaches about all who reject the matchless grace of God as offered through His Son, Jesus Christ.

A pastor was asked to officiate at a funeral for a man who spent his entire life addicted to alcohol. The man's constant use of alcohol led him to abuse everyone around him physically and emotionally. Even as he lay on his deathbed, he rejected every attempt by his family to talk to him about his soul. When he died, the family decided to have a brief graveside service, and they asked this pastor to speak. Some of the family members attended the church the pastor served, and the family insisted that he tell those in attendance that their father was in hell. The pastor reluctantly preached a message from Luke 16:19–31 (the story of the rich man and Lazarus) where he focused on the fact there is, "a great chasm" between the living and the dead. He reminded everyone that like heaven, hell is forever. There is no relief, reprieve, or possibility of restoration. He told those standing by the open grave that hell is the destination of all who refuse the grace and mercy of God provided in Christ. He then presented the gospel, telling everyone how they could escape the eternal destruction of hell by repenting, confessing their sin, and trusting in Jesus for salvation. He said no one responded that day (they were probably in shock that a preacher was actually talking about hell at a funeral!) but hopefully the message became a seed in their hearts that will one day bear the fruit of salvation.

Simply stated, hell is eternal separation from God. Jesus talked more about hell than just about any other subject.

One of the Greek words that translates "hell" is *Gehenna*. In 1999 I (Tony), along with my wife, spent two weeks in Israel. We spent the first week touring the area of Galilee and the second week touring the area around Jerusalem and the Dead Sea. While we were in Jerusalem, we stayed at a hotel on the Mount of Olives. When we walked out on our balcony, we could see the Eastern Gate of the city. Below us was the garden of Gethsemane, and to the left of the walls of the city was the valley of Gehenna. Today, it is a beautiful park filled with green grass and flowering trees. In Jesus's day, it was the trash dump of the city, and it was constantly burning or smoldering. Smoke and flames rose constantly as people would bring their refuse to the Dung Gate and deposit it into the perpetual burning of the valley of Gehenna. I can imagine Jesus pointing to this awful sight as He used the word Gehenna to describe the final resting place for the devil, his angels, and all who reject the saving grace of God in Christ.

Jesus spoke parables about the separation of the saved and lost. One such account is found in Matthew 25, where Jesus referred to the saved as the sheep and the lost as the goats. Jesus said God will place the sheep on His right side and the goats on His left. "Then the King will say to those on his right, 'Come, you who are blessed by my Father, inherit the kingdom prepared for you from the foundation of the world. . . . Then he will say to those on his left, 'Depart from me, you cursed, into the eternal fire prepared for the devil and his angels'" (Matthew 25:34, 41 ESV). Those who have been made righteous through Jesus's atonement will be welcomed into a prepared Kingdom of eternal life, love, and light in the presence of God. Those who reject Jesus will be cast into the horror of everlasting fire and torment. Both final destinations, heaven and hell, are eternal states where, for the saved, there is no threat of losing the eternal blessings of God; and for the lost, there is no hope of release from the eternal curse of refusing God's grace.

In many places the Bible clearly states that just as heaven is eternal life and blessing, hell is eternal death and destruction. For example:

- Multitudes who sleep in the dust of the earth will awake: some to everlasting life, others to shame and everlasting contempt. (Daniel 12:2)

- "Then they will go away to eternal punishment, but the righteous to eternal life." (Matthew 25:46)

- They will be punished with everlasting destruction and shut out from the presence of the Lord and from the glory of his might. (2 Thessalonians 1:9)

- And the devil, who deceived them, was thrown into the lake of burning sulfur, where the beast and the false prophet had been thrown. They will be tormented day and night forever and ever. . . . Anyone whose name was not found written in the book of life was thrown into the lake of fire. (Revelation 20:10, 15)

The forever nature of our final destination should motivate every believer to urgently and passionately share the gospel with the lost.

Some people use the words *hades* and *hell* interchangeably. However, they are not the same. The New Testament refers to hades as the place of the dead. The story of the rich man and Lazarus in Luke 16 suggests that hades (this place of the dead) is divided into two very different states of existence. "Now the poor man died and was carried away by the angels to Abraham's bosom; and the rich man also died and was buried. In Hades he lifted up his eyes, being in torment, and saw Abraham far away and Lazarus in his bosom" (Luke 16:22–23 NASB). Before Jesus died on the cross, no one, not even the Old Testament saints, could enter into the perfect presence of God. When the righteous of the Old Testament died they went to paradise or "the bosom of Abraham." When the unrighteous died they went to "torment" where they suffer while waiting for the final judgment. Many scholars believe when Jesus told the thief on the cross who asked Him for mercy, "Today you will be with me in paradise," He was talking about the place of the righteous dead referenced in Luke 16. But Jesus didn't stay long in paradise. In fact, when He entered paradise, He "led a host of captives, / and he gave gifts to men" (Ephesians 4:8 ESV). Paul goes on in this passage to say, "In saying, 'He ascended,' what does it mean but that he had also descended into the lower regions, the earth? He who descended is the one who also ascended far above all the heavens, that he might fill all things" (Ephesians 4:9–10 ESV).

What does all this mean? It means when Jesus died, He went to paradise and revealed Himself to the righteous dead of the Old Testament. Once Jesus poured out His blood for our atonement, the way to heaven was opened, and He led the righteous dead out of paradise (which is now empty) into the presence of God, leaving the unrighteous dead to suffer in torment while awaiting their final judgment as described in Revelation 20:

> Then I saw a great white throne and Him who sat on it, from whose face the earth and heaven fled away. And there was found no place for them. And I saw the dead, small and great, standing before God, and books were opened. And another book was opened, which is the Book of Life. And the dead were judged according to their works, by the things which were written in the books. The sea gave up the dead who were in it, and Death and Hades delivered up the dead who were in them. And they were judged, each one according to his works. Then Death and Hades were cast into the lake of fire. This is the second death. And anyone not found written in the Book of Life was cast into the lake of fire. (verses 11–15 NKJV)

Life Answers

In this short study of the afterlife, we see the Bible teaches about two places where people spend eternity. Heaven is wonderful beyond our limited ability to comprehend. Likewise, hell transcends the bounds of our understanding of pain and suffering. The thought of heaven should cause believers to rejoice and to take hope that death is only the beginning of an eternal state of bliss. The thought of hell should cause us to take the good news of Jesus Christ to everyone we know. If you have not received Jesus as your Savior, I implore you to stop reading, confess your sins, and surrender your life to Christ.

Points to Remember

1. There are two destinations after death: heaven and hell. Both are forever.

2. There are different types of *heavens* mentioned in the Bible.

3. Believers' spirits go to be with God in heaven upon death.

4. Believers will inherit the new earth with their new and glorified resurrected bodies.

5. Hell is a place of torment for those who have rejected Jesus Christ.

6. Nonbelievers go to hell upon death and will eventually inherit the lake of fire.

7. The truth of hell should move us to share the gospel with as many people as possible.

Notes

[1] Woody Allen, "Death, A Play" in *Without Feathers* (New York: Ballantine Books, 1983), 106.

[2] See also Psalm 57:11; 102:25; Nehemiah 9:6; 2 Corinthians 12:2–4.

[3] See also Matthew 6:9–10; 18:10.

Chapter 11

How Does Christianity Compare with Other Religions?

How Is Christianity Different?

"Salvation is found in no one else, for there is no other name under heaven given to mankind by which we must be saved."
— Acts 4:12

In today's culture many people have embraced a postmodern worldview that teaches truth is subjective and morality is relative. David Dockery, in his book *The Challenge of Postmodernism* defines postmodernism as "a disbelief in objective truth and a deep sense that morality is relative."[1] Individuals who claim to know or possess truth are subjected to a high degree of skepticism. Anyone who has the boldness to believe and teach his or her religion as the only true religion is considered to be bigoted and intellectually narrow. In this environment it should come as no surprise that a growing number of people are making statements such as "Well, all religions are the same," or worse, "All religions lead to God."

To say that all religions are the same reduces devoutly held beliefs to little more than a simple moral code that can be followed or ignored based on the circumstances of the moment (moment-by-moment reality). Christianity consists

125

of and proclaims many absolute truth statements that are incompatible with and cannot be reconciled to the truth claims of other religions. The Quran teaches Muslims to destroy the opponents of Islam (Sura 5:33), whereas the Bible teaches Christians to love their enemies (Matthew 5:44). That one statement alone reveals a huge disparity between the two religions. Buddhists do not believe in sin, yet the Bible teaches that "all have sinned and fall short of the glory of God" (Romans 3:23). Again, a stark contrast exists between these two religions. A simple survey of the major tenets of the world's religious systems renders any statement that all religions are the same to be untenable.

A far greater problem than the idea that all religions are the same is the idea that all religions lead to God (Universalism). Why is this so bad? To say that all religions lead to God means all the gods of the different religions will lead to the same thing, whether that "thing" is a god or spirit or just consciousness, as New Age spiritualists believe. Therefore, to say that all religions lead to God is to ignore the first of the Ten Commandments, "You shall have no other gods before Me" (Exodus 20:3 NKJV). Later, Moses also wrote, "Hear, O Israel: The LORD our God, the LORD is one" (Deuteronomy 6:4 NKJV). Monotheism, the belief that there is only one God, is shared by the three major religions of the world. Christianity, Islam, and Judaism all confess one God; however, all three have a very different view of the nature of God. Christianity, as discussed earlier, is Trinitarian in its teaching of the nature of God, which means God exists as one with three divine manifestations all existing at the same time.

Since all religions diverge at many points of understanding, what makes Christianity the true religion? The simple answer is *Jesus*! Jesus Christ is the true distinction of Christianity that separates it from the other religions. So to discover how Christianity compares with other religions, we will look at Jesus Himself, because without Jesus Christianity loses its distinctiveness. Unfortunately, Christianity, as expressed by many who merely claim the name of Jesus, has been plagued with scandal and bloodshed for more than two thousand years. People who believed they were acting in the name of Christianity have been guilty of terrible atrocities. But Jesus Christ and the interpretation of God's Word in the power of the Holy Spirit leads us to a true understanding of the nature of Christianity. Similarly, rather than looking at the followers of other religions, we will focus on their founders. How is Jesus different from other religious figures throughout history? Why do those differences make Jesus's way the true way? These questions will be answered in this chapter.

Jesus Was Sinless

Jesus Christ is the only sinless person who ever lived. Most founders of other faiths would not be so audacious as to claim perfection, yet Jesus lived a perfect life without sin. This separates Him from any other founder of a religious system. Consider these other religions and their views of sin.

Anyone who claims sinlessness in the Hindu faith cannot be a true Hindu. A sinless founder would be an impossible concept for a Hindu because a true Hindu must be sinful. If he is not sinful, he will be released out of the Wheel of Samsara[2] into Brahman[3] and will not return to the earth or reality as we know it.

Similarly, Buddha taught that the path to enlightenment would release someone from the illusion of this life into nirvana, or a state of nonexistence. In other words, the hope of the Buddhist is to become so enlightened that the person simply ceases to exist. To the Buddhist, sinlessness can only exist when the person ceases to exist.

Muhammad, the founder of Islam, actually asked for Allah's forgiveness three times in the Quran, while stating that Jesus was the only pure, or sinless, man to have lived! Even Muhammad knew there was something special about Jesus!

The following verses describe Jesus's sinlessness:

- God made him who had no sin to be sin for us, so that in him we might become the righteousness of God. (2 Corinthians 5:21)

- "He committed no sin, / and no deceit was found in his mouth." (1 Peter 2:22)

- For we do not have a high priest who is unable to empathize with our weaknesses, but we have one who has been tempted in every way, just as we are—yet he did not sin. (Hebrews 4:15)

- But you know that he appeared so that he might take away our sins. And in him is no sin. (1 John 3:5)

- How much more, then, will the blood of Christ, who through the eternal Spirit offered himself unblemished to

God, cleanse our consciences from acts that lead to death, so that we may serve the living God! (Hebrews 9:14)

- But with the precious blood of Christ, a lamb without blemish or defect. (1 Peter 1:19)

Jesus's nature was sinless, something that no other founder of faith could or would claim!

Jesus Is the Savior

In his book, *Christ Among Other Gods*,[4] Erwin Lutzer shares a heartbreaking story about a grandmother and her two-year-old granddaughter. The grandmother was taking care of her little granddaughter one day, and they were playing by the pool. The little girl accidentally fell in the pool and started to drown. The grandmother immediately jumped in the pool to try to rescue her granddaughter. The only problem was that the grandmother did not know how to swim. Though it would be nice to tell you that the grandmother succeeded in saving the granddaughter, or even gave her life to save the granddaughter, it is simply not true. The grandmother and the granddaughter both died that day.

This story illustrates the simple fact that just because people have the will to save someone else, it does not mean they are able to. This is what separates Jesus Christ from the founders of other faiths. Though He may not be the only one with a desire to save human beings, He is the only one who is able to save us! No other major religious figure has claimed to be the Savior. They have given instructions to others on how to save themselves or pointed to a way that would eventually lead to salvation. Jesus Christ stated clearly He did not come to *show* the path to salvation but to *be* the path to salvation for all who would follow Him.

Jesus said, "The Son of Man has come to seek and to save that which was lost" (Luke 19:10 NKJV), and "I am the way, the truth, and the life. No one comes to the Father except through me" (John 14:6 NKJV). No other teachers claimed to be able to save their followers. Jesus stands distinctly alone in this group as the only one who can and will save all who repent of their sins and place their trust in Him. Jesus Christ is the only person to live sinlessly, qualifying Himself to be our Savior and to impute His righteousness to us!

Jesus Brought God to Us

One of the names given to Jesus is Immanuel. The name *Immanuel*, means, "God, with us." Jesus offered to do what no other founder of any other faith offered to do or could do—He brought God to us. Paul said,

> Have this mind among yourselves, which is yours in Christ Jesus, who, though he was in the form of God, did not count equality with God a thing to be grasped, but emptied himself, by taking the form of a servant, being born in the likeness of men. And being found in human form, he humbled himself by becoming obedient to the point of death, even death on a cross. (Philippians 2:5–8 ESV)

This scripture says that Jesus Christ, though in the form of God, emptied Himself to be born in human form. In that way, Christ brought God to us in a way no other faith founder could hope to match.

Buddhism, Confucianism, and other similar Eastern religions all promote an ethical lifestyle. They are technically atheistic in nature and practice. So, of course, the early leaders of Buddhism would never have claimed to bring God to their followers.

Muhammad, especially, would not have claimed to have brought God to his followers. He was disgusted with what he considered to be idolatry during his time and set out to purge the world. The cardinal belief is that Allah is one, and the cardinal sin is to ascribe divinity to anyone else. For Muhammad to have claimed to share the nature of Allah would have been the greatest blasphemy imaginable.

Christ is unique in that He brings God to us through the incarnation. Read again the message of the angel Gabriel as he revealed God's incredible plan to His servant Mary:

> "Do not be afraid, Mary; for you have found favor with God. And behold, you will conceive in your womb and bear a son, and you shall name Him Jesus. He will be great and will be called the Son of the Most High; and the Lord God will give Him the throne of His father David; and He will reign over the house of Jacob forever, and His kingdom will have no end." Mary said to the angel, "How can this be, since I am a virgin?" The angel answered and said to her, "The Holy Spirit will come upon you, and the power of the Most High will overshadow you; and for that reason, the holy Child shall be called the Son of God." (Luke 1:30–35 NASB)

Jesus's teachings, His life, His miracles, and (most notable) His resurrection give proof to His oneness with the Father. On this topic, C.S. Lewis wrote:

> There is no half-way house and there is no parallel in other religions. If you had gone to Buddha and asked him "Are you the son of Brahmah?" he would have said, "My son, you are still in the vale of illusion." If you had gone to Socrates and asked, "Are you Zeus?" he would have laughed at you. If you had gone to Mohammed and asked, "Are you Allah?" he would first have rent his clothes and then cut your head off.[5]

Simply stated, no other teacher can claim to have brought God to us.

Jesus Defeated Death

Perhaps the greatest distinction between Jesus and the founders of other faiths is His defeat of death through His resurrection. Paul's writings capture and communicate the power of the resurrection in many places in the New Testament, but perhaps nowhere better than Colossians 2:13–15:

> When you were dead in your sins and in the uncircumcision of your flesh, God made you alive with Christ. He forgave us all our sins, having canceled the charge of our legal indebtedness, which stood against us and condemned us; he has taken it away, nailing it to the cross. And having disarmed the powers and authorities, he made a public spectacle of them, triumphing over them by the cross.

Though many people might claim that the resurrection was false, chapter 6 discusses all of the evidence that proves the resurrection to be true. Therefore, the fact the resurrection is true proves that Jesus is the only person to have defeated death. Buddha's bones are scattered and enshrined in different places. Muhammad's bones are located in Medina. The bones of Jesus have never been found and will never be found because He defeated death and rose from the grave.

One of the greatest things about Jesus's having been raised from the dead is His prophecy of the resurrection. Matthew 16:21 records, "From that time on Jesus began to explain to his disciples that he must go to Jerusalem and suffer many things at the hands of the elders, the chief priests and the teachers of the law, and that he must be killed and on the third day be raised to life" (see also Mark 8:31). Also, referring to His body, Jesus answered the scribes and Pharisees, "Destroy this temple, and I will raise it again in three days" (John 2:19; see also Mark 14:58). Jesus declared boldly in John 10:17–18, "The reason my Father loves me is that I lay down my life—only to take it up again. No one takes it from me, but I lay it down of my own accord. I have authority to lay it down and authority to take it up again." Jesus proclaimed over and over again that He would willingly sacrifice His life and then rise from the dead. He did . . . and that one fact separates Jesus and therefore Christianity from every other religion.

Life Answers

Jesus separates Himself from other faith founders in many different ways; and since Christianity is founded upon His teachings and claims, true Christianity is distinguished from other religions because of Jesus—who He is, what He did, and what He will do. One final distinction between Jesus and all other religious leaders is that Jesus promised He would return. Jesus said, "Therefore you also be ready, for the Son of Man is coming at an hour you do not expect" (Luke 12:40 NKJV). When Jesus ascended into heaven, the disciples who were with Him stood and stared as He disappeared gradually from their sight. They were still standing and staring when two angels appeared and said, "Men of Galilee, why do you stand gazing up into heaven? This same Jesus, who was taken up from you into heaven, will so come in like manner as you saw Him go into heaven" (Acts 1:11 NKJV). All other religious adherents are hoping and praying they have done enough to make it into their version of paradise. Christians all over the world, resting in the blessed assurance of our salvation through the imputed righteousness of Christ, are watching and waiting for our Lord's return!

Points to Remember

1. No one can say, "All religions lead to God" or "All religions are the same" and be correct.

2. Jesus distinguishes Christianity from other religions.

3. Jesus is the only sinless faith founder.

4. Jesus is the only faith founder who qualifies to be Savior.

5. Jesus is the only faith founder who brought God to humanity.

6. Jesus is the only faith founder who defeated death.

Notes

[1] David S. Dockery, ed., *The Challenge of Postmodernism* (Grand Rapids, MI: Baker Book House, 2001), 12.

[2] The Wheel of Samsara is a Hindu concept that refers to the cycles of life a person experiences in a lifetime.

[3] Brahman is the closest concept of God a Hindu has. It is essentially the ultimate reality in which everything exists.

[4] Erwin W. Lutzer, "An Extraordinary Birth," *Christ among Other Gods* (Chicago, IL: Moody Publishers, 2016), 73.

[5] C.S. Lewis, *God in the Dock: Essays on Theology and Ethics*, ed. Walter Hooper (Grand Rapids, MI: William B. Eerdmans, 2014), 168.

Chapter 12

Why Does God Allow Suffering and Evil?

The Truth about God's Role

Dear friends, do not be surprised at the fiery ordeal that has come on you to test you, as though something strange were happening to you. But rejoice inasmuch as you participate in the sufferings of Christ, so that you may be overjoyed when his glory is revealed. — 1 Peter 4:12–13

In the Old Testament, the book of Amos uses the analogy of a man who flees from a lion only to meet a bear. He then flees from the bear, eventually making it home; but as he leans against the wall inside his home to rest, a snake bites him (5:19). Have you ever felt like the man in this story? Calamity comes, and you do your best to avoid it only to discover many circumstances in life are inevitable and unavoidable.

Evil and suffering are part of the inevitable and unavoidable circumstances of life. Living in this world means you will encounter both, and they are frequently linked together. The existence of evil and suffering creates many problems for believers and nonbelievers alike when we consider the existence and benevolence of God. The Bible clearly teaches that God is good, and no doubt anyone who has chosen to follow

Christ would agree that God's love is far beyond comprehension. God's goodness is never questioned when things are going well, but as soon as the bills become difficult to pay, a child dies, or a terrorist group kills hundreds, God's goodness becomes open to scrutiny and doubt.

Thankfully, God addresses this problem in the Bible. He has revealed through the writers He inspired how evil in the world and the goodness of God can exist at the same time. The argument presented by many skeptics against God's goodness goes something like this:

If God is good, naturally He would want to eliminate evil.

If God is all-powerful, He should be able to eliminate evil.

If God is all-knowing, He must know how to eliminate evil.

Evil has no redeeming purpose, so why does God allow evil to exist?

With all of this in mind, let's consider the primary explanations for the coexistence of God's goodness and the world's evil.

God Permits Evil to Bring about a Greater Good

James tells us, "Consider it all joy, my brethren, when you encounter various trials, knowing that the testing of your faith produces endurance. And let endurance have its perfect result, so that you may be perfect and compete, lacking in nothing" (James 1:2–4 NASB). Though suffering and evil are painful, they can sometimes be the greatest experiences a Christian can have through his or her walk with Jesus. Trials and testing that rise from the presence of evil in the world are tools in the hands of a loving God, who uses them to shape us more into His image. In this case, James reveals that God uses trials and testing to produce endurance, which leads to our being made complete.

Perhaps the best illustration from the Old Testament of this truth is the story of Joseph. If you grew up with siblings, you may be able to relate to Joseph's dilemma. He experienced sibling rivalry in the extreme when his brothers, who were jealous of the affection Joseph received from his father and angry at the arrogance they perceived when Joseph told them about his dream where his whole family bowed down to him, tossed him in an open well with the intent of killing him. When they saw a passing caravan of Midianite traders, they decided to sell him into slavery rather than take his life. Joseph ended up in Egypt, where he was unjustly accused of trying to rape his master's wife. He was sent to prison, and he languished for ten years until Pharaoh needed someone to interpret a disturbing dream. Joseph rightly interpreted Pharaoh's dream, and Pharaoh rewarded Joseph by making him the second most powerful person in Egypt. When a great famine drove Joseph's brothers to leave their home and travel to Egypt for food to survive, they were reunited with their brother, whom I am sure they believed was dead. Joseph's brothers were afraid when they recognized him because they could see he was a powerful leader in Egypt, and they knew he held their lives in his hands. What would

Joseph do? Would he lash out in anger and exact revenge? Would he forgive and forget? Genesis 45:4–5 gives us the answer. "Then Joseph said to his brothers, 'Come close to me.' When they had done so, he said, 'I am your brother Joseph, the one you sold into Egypt! And now, do not be distressed and do not be angry with yourselves for selling me here, because it was to save lives that God sent me ahead of you.'"

God used the trials and testing of Joseph's life to put him in a place where he could save the lives of his family members and so he could save many lives in Egypt from famine. God can and often does take the evil we do and turn it into an opportunity for our good and His glory. Paul put it this way: "And we know that for those who love God all things work together for good, for those who are called according to his purpose" (Romans 8:28 ESV). Paul is certainly not saying all things are good. He is saying that when the entirety of God's plan is revealed, we can see (and sometimes we can't see but must trust) that the good things and the bad things are united in the everlasting lovingkindness of our heavenly Father.

My (Tony's) dad spent forty years, almost his entire working life, as a paint contractor. At one time he employed as many as twelve painters and operated two industrial airless spray systems. I used to work with him in the summer, and I was always fascinated with the process of mixing several colors of paint together to make a new color. Today, that process is done digitally by a computer program with just the right amount of the different colors being added. Back then, the only computer program was my dad's experience! He would pour several different colors into a gallon bucket of "base white" paint. When each of the colors was poured in, it left a mark, a dot of the color on the surface of the base white. The white looked unaffected by the addition of the different colors, but when Dad would take a paint stick and begin to stir the paint together, it immediately began to transform into the desired color.

Every time I think about seeing my dad mixing paint the old fashioned way, I am reminded of Romans 8:28. The different colors poured into the base white left their marks, seemingly marring the purity of the base white. But the moment my dad stirred the paint, what once appeared to be marred became something new and beautiful. That is how God works in our lives. Sometimes, something comes into our lives that appears to mar the beauty of the way God made us. Some situation or event leaves a mark that is painful. But then God begins to move, and when He "stirs the bucket" in a way that makes all things come together for good, the result is something new and beautiful.

Human Beings Have Some Measure of Free Will and Are Affected by the Fall

The garden of Eden was a perfect world that was free from sin, with all things operating under the sovereignty of God. But Adam and Eve rebelled against God's perfect order. Eve was tempted and gave in to the enticements of the serpent. Genesis 3:6 describes Eve's reasoning concerning the forbidden fruit of the tree in the midst of the garden. "When the woman saw that the fruit of the tree was good for food and pleasing to the eye, and also desirable for gaining wisdom, she took some and ate it. She also gave some to her husband, who was with her, and he ate it." To sin is to substitute our will in the place of God's will. It is the arrogance of believing our way is better than His way. Rebellion against God calls the nature and character of God into question, and it is a product of our sinful inclination to elevate our desire above His divine plan.

The sin of Adam and Eve has been passed down to all humanity. Paul wrote, "Therefore, just as through one man sin entered into the world, and death through sin, and so death spread to all men, because all sinned" (Romans 5:12 NASB). Later, in the same chapter, he added, "So then as through one transgression there resulted condemnation to all men, even so through one act of righteousness there resulted justification of life to all men" (verse 18 NASB).

Adam and Eve exercised their ability to make a moral choice, and they chose to disobey God, leaving all of creation affected by the ravages of sin. Once Adam and Eve sinned, the stage was set for humanity to choose between that which is morally good (in line with God's ways) and that which is evil (in line with the rebellion of the serpent). A complete discussion of the biblical evidence for God allowing humans to exercise free will is beyond the scope of this book. However, when considering free will within the discussion of the existence of evil, we need to realize that if our choosing to serve God honors Him, brings Him glory, and results in our ultimate good, then we must concede the opposite is also true. Choosing to ignore God's law and rebel against Him and His Word brings evil instead of God's glory into the world. So whether we choose to praise Him or deny Him, our choice matters because we are held accountable for that choice. To believe otherwise is to make God the author of evil, which Scripture clearly says is false. John tells us, "This is the message we have heard from him and proclaim to you, that God is light, and in him is no darkness at all" (1 John 1:5 ESV). James also reminds us, "Let no one say when he is tempted, 'I am being tempted by God,' for God cannot be tempted with evil, and he himself tempts no one" (James 1:13 ESV).

What can we conclude from this? (1) God is not the author of evil because there is no evil associated with Him. He is pure light, existing without the slightest taint of darkness. (2) God is not the author of evil because He is not the one who tempts us. Speaking again about temptation, James said, "But each person is tempted when he is lured and enticed by his own desire. Then desire when it has conceived gives birth to sin, and sin when it is fully grown brings forth death" (James 1:14–15 ESV).

Do you see the progression? Satan places the temptation before us. We are lured into succumbing to the temptation because our fallen nature is attracted to it. If we follow sin to its logical conclusion, it leads to death. Peter tells us, "Be sober-minded; be watchful. Your adversary the devil prowls around like a roaring lion, seeking someone to devour" (1 Peter 5:8 ESV). Satan is a devourer. He brings death and destruction in his wake for all who are enticed and carried away by temptation.

So, if God is not the author of evil, then Satan is the tempter, and it is our own fallen nature that leads us to give in to the temptation to do evil. The presence of evil in the world must be attributed to our moral choice to follow after the temptation and rebel against God.

The Universe Has a Natural Order

Some persons explain evil by suggesting that God created a world where good and evil rise from the natural, created order. For example, water that sustains life can also take a life by means of drowning and destroy property by means of flooding. Fire provides warmth, heat, and light; but a fire out of control brings destruction and death. The sun gives light and warmth that allows life to be sustained on earth; but it can also, if not balanced by rain, bring drought that leads to destruction.

Many Eastern-based religious systems cling to an understanding of good and evil that suggests good must have evil to exist and evil must have good to exist. This view is not biblical because it places good and evil on equal footing with the ultimate outcome in doubt. God's Word affirms in many places the supremacy of God and Christ, but perhaps none better than Paul's description of what Christ accomplished on the cross. "And you, who were dead in your trespasses and the uncircumcision of your flesh, God made alive together with him, having forgiven us all our trespasses, by canceling the record of debt that stood against us with its legal demands. This he set aside, nailing it to the cross. He disarmed the rulers and authorities and put them to open shame, by *triumphing over them in him*" (Colossians 2:13–15 ESV, emphasis mine).

Darkness has no power over light. No one has ever walked into a pitch dark room, flipped on a light switch, and heard the darkness exclaim, "No, I'm not going!" Immediately at the flip of the switch, darkness is dispelled and light fills the room. In the same way, good is not merely the other side of the evil coin. Goodness, holiness, light, and righteousness are all characteristics of God; and once Satan, who is already defeated, is destroyed, only the characteristics of God will remain.

John, in the book of Revelation says,

> Then I saw an angel coming down from heaven, having the key to the bottomless pit and a great chain in his hand. He laid hold of the dragon, that serpent of old, who is the Devil and Satan, and bound him for a thousand years; and he cast him into the bottomless pit, and shut him up, and set a seal on him, so that he should deceive the nations no more till the thousand years were finished. But after these things he must be released for a little while (20:1–3 NKJV).

I (Tony) have often preached that when Jesus comes I know exactly where I want Him to find me. Can you guess where? I want to be right next to the angel that binds Satan so that maybe I can get a good swift kick in as he is cast into the pit! Evil will one day be defeated, and God will actually send an angel to take care of Satan when the time comes. There is no comparison between the power of evil and the supreme goodness and unmatched power of God.

God Transforms Our Pain into Soul-making

What is soul-making? In modern athletic terms we might call it the "no pain, no gain" principle. In other words, God will often allow tests and challenges to come into our lives, and then He uses those tests and challenges to mold and shape us more into the image of His Son, Jesus Christ. We see this principle expressed by James: "Count it all joy, my brothers, when you meet trials of various kinds, for you know that the testing of your faith produces steadfastness. And let steadfastness have its full effect, that you may be perfect and complete, lacking in nothing" (James 1:2–4 ESV). God uses our trials, troubles, challenges, and even our pain to make us complete so that we lack nothing.

Not long after I trusted Christ as my Savior, He called me into full-time Christian service. To prepare, God called me to go to Southeastern Baptist Theological Seminary in Wake Forest, North Carolina. My wife (Denise) and I had two small children at home, and I was going to give up a very lucrative job to attend seminary full-time for at least three years. God knew Denise and I both would need a great amount of faith in His ability to provide for us if we were going to make it through this challenge. So, about three months before I was scheduled to start driving four hours to Southeastern on Monday and four hours to get back home on Friday, God allowed a trial to come into our lives. Our daughter Amber was diagnosed with a joint disorder that involved her ball and socket hip joint. She had just started walking, and every time she took a step, we could hear a clicking sound. X-rays confirmed that the ball and socket

had not fully formed, and she would have to endure correc-
tive surgery. Our faces went white as the doctor described
the surgery telling us that she would be in a body cast for approximately three months. They even talked about fashion-
ing a handle on the back part of the cast so we could move
her around!

Denise was devastated, and I was angry. I couldn't believe God would throw this curve into our lives right at the
moment I was going to sacrifice to serve Him! I prayed for
a miracle, but I confess I had bitterness in my heart that
God would allow this trial at this particular time. We prayed
about this over the weekend, and neither one of us had peace
about proceeding with the surgery. We asked if we could get
a second opinion. The second doctor concurred the problem would have to be addressed, but he agreed to wait three
months and check her again.

The week before I was scheduled to leave to go to Wake
Forest, Denise took Amber back to see if there was any change
in her condition. The doctor ordered the X-rays and called
Denise in for the final verdict. When Denise went into the
room, the doctor had placed the X-rays on the display, but he
didn't turn the light on so she could see the results. Instead,
he asked her if she had noticed anything unusual about Amber. Denise didn't want to tell him that yes, Amber had been
throwing her leg out to the side when she walked. Denise was
sure that was a bad sign and would mean the surgery would
have to be put on the schedule. But the doctor smiled as he
turned the light on behind the X-rays. On one side was the
orginal X-ray clearly showing the deformed ball and socket
joint. On the other side was an X-ray of a perfectly formed ball

and socket joint! He asked Denise when Amber began throwing her leg out to the side when she walked, and Denise told him it was right after our visit with the first doctor. The doctor said, "That was the Lord—when Amber started throwing her leg out as she walked, it pushed the ball up into the socket the same way the cast would have worked! I would have to say that God intervened and healed your daughter! You can take her home—the surgery won't be necessary."

Needless to say we were both humbled and overjoyed. God used the trial of facing an almost impossible situation with our daughter to increase our faith by showing us His power. It was a soul-making experience that sustained us through many challenging days while I was in seminary.

Henri Nouwen wrote in his book *The Wounded Healer,* "Perhaps the main task of the minister is to prevent people from suffering for the wrong reasons."[1] In this sense, the first thing to understand is that God actually does use suffering. Too often, people ask why God would allow something or why God did something. Unfortunately, many Christians do not understand that God never wastes suffering. Do not confuse this with the idea that God causes all suffering. God did not cause Job's suffering, Satan did. Nevertheless, God did not allow Job's suffering to leave him barren. Job's suffering bore fruit by revealing to him the power, majesty, and ultimately the sovereignty of God.

Perhaps the greatest reward and reasons for suffering is captured in Paul's epistle to the Philippian church:

> But whatever things were gain to me, those things I have counted as loss for the sake of Christ. More than that, I

count all things to be loss in view of the *surpassing value of knowing Christ Jesus my Lord*, for whom I have suffered the loss of *all* things, and count them but rubbish so that I may *gain Christ, and may be found in Him,* . . . that I may know Him and the power of His resurrection and *the fellowship of His sufferings*, being conformed to His death (Philippians 3:7–10 NASB, emphasis mine).

Paul said it was through suffering that he knew Christ, and that knowing Christ surpassed all other things in worth. Paul's reward was knowing Christ and being found in Him, and Paul would rather suffer to know Christ than to prosper and not know Christ.

There is a certain maturity in Paul's statement that sometimes takes a while to reach. However, his statement teaches that suffering can be used to know Christ in a way that nothing else can. After all, the writer of Hebrews said that Christ endured all suffering so that He can understand and empathize with our suffering. "Therefore, in all things [Christ] had to be made like His brethren . . . For in that He Himself has suffered, being tempted, He is able to aid those who are tempted" (Hebrews 2:17–18 NKJV). Just two chapters later he says again, "For we do not have a High Priest who cannot sympathize with our weaknesses, but was in all points tempted as we are, yet without sin" (Hebrews 4:15 NKJV). Since Jesus endured suffering to help those who suffer, it only makes sense that we can know Christ more deeply through suffering.

Life Answers

Evil and suffering are both issues that create doubt and disbelief in God. Yet we need not fear evil because it provides us with an ability to love God genuinely; and though evil is difficult to endure at times, it is often during the worst evil that we can experience the love of God the most. We should pray that suffering and evil cause us to cling closer to God instead of driving us away. Also, remember that suffering exists because God allows humanity to choose between God and evil, yet suffering is allowed because it perfects the children of God.

Points to Remember

1. Evil and suffering came into existence by Adam's choice to sin.

2. Sin is a result of the free will that God gave humans so that those who love God can love Him genuinely.

3. Suffering is used by God but not caused by God.

4. Suffering is used to perfect the saint.

5. Suffering is used to drawer us deeper into an intimate relationship with Jesus Christ.

Notes

[1] Henri J. M. Nouwen, *The Wounded Healer: Ministry in Contemporary Society* (New York: Doubleday, 1979), 93.

Appendix*

How to Begin a Personal Relationship with Jesus Christ

If you have not yet entered into a personal relationship with Jesus Christ, we encourage you to make this wonderful discovery today. This very simple acrostic—L.I.F.E.—will explain, knowing that God wants you to not only inherit *eternal* life but also to experience *eternal* life to its fullest.

L = Love

It all begins with God's love. God created you in His image. This means you were created to live in relationship with Him. *"For God so loved the world, that He gave His only begotten Son, that whoever believes in Him shall not perish, but have eternal life"* (John 3:16).

But if God loves you and desires a relationship with you, why do you feel so isolated from Him?

I = Isolation

This isolation is created by our sin—our rebellion against God—which separates us from Him and from others. *"For all have sinned and fall short of the glory of God"* (Romans 3:23). *"For the wages of sin is death, but the free gift of God is eternal life in Christ Jesus our Lord"* (Romans 6:23).

You might wonder how you can overcome this isolation and have an intimate relationship with God.

F = Forgiveness

The only solution to humanity's isolation and separation from a holy God is forgiveness. *"For Christ also died for sins once for all, the just for the unjust, so that He might bring us to God, having been put to death in the flesh, but made alive in the spirit"* (1 Peter 3:18).

The only way our relationship with God can be restored is through the forgiveness of our sins. Jesus Christ died on the cross for this very purpose.

E = Eternal Life

You can have a full and abundant life in this present life . . . and eternal life when you die. *"But as many as received Him, to them He gave the right to become children of God, even to those who believe in His name"* (John 1:12). *"The thief comes only to steal and kill and destroy; I came that they may have life, and have it abundantly"* (John 10:10).

Is there any reason you wouldn't like to have a personal relationship with God?

The Plan of Salvation

It's as simple as ABC. All you have to do is:

A = Admit you are a sinner.

Turn from your sin and turn to God. *"Repent and return, so that your sins may be wiped away, in order that times of refreshing may come from the presence of the Lord"* (Acts 3:19).

B = Believe that Jesus died for your sins and rose from the dead, enabling you to have life.

"These things I have written to you who believe in the name of the Son of God, so that you know that you have eternal life" (1 John 5:13).

C= Confess verbally and publicly your belief in Jesus Christ.

"If you confess with your mouth Jesus as Lord, and believe in your heart that God raised Him from the dead, you will be saved; for with the heart a person believes, resulting in righteousness, and with the mouth he confesses, resulting in salvation" (Romans 10:9–10).

You can invite Jesus Christ to come into your life right now. Pray something like this:

> "God, I admit that I am a sinner. I believe that you sent Jesus, who died on the cross and rose from the dead, paying the penalty for my sins. I am asking that you forgive me of my sin, and I receive your gift of eternal life. It is in Jesus's name that I ask for this gift. Amen."

Signed _____

Date _____

If you have a friend or family member who is a Christian, tell that person about your decision. Then find a church that teaches the Bible, and let them help you go deeper with Christ.

May God bless you as you journey on with Him.

If you made a decision for Christ just now, it would be an honor to hear from you. If you have questions or spiritual needs, write to us at:

North Greenville University
PO Box 1892
Tigerville, SC 29688

* Scriptures in the Appendix are taken from the New American Standard version of the Bible.

About the Authors

Tony Beam is vice president of Student Life and Christian Worldview at North Greenville University, located near Greenville, South Carolina. Founded in 1892, North Greenville is a nationally known, rapidly growing institution dedicated to the Great Commission and to the historic Christian faith. Dr. Beam has served as a pastor, educator, and broadcaster, hosting *Christian Worldview Today*, a favorite morning drive-time show heard in the Carolinas. www.christiantalk660.com.

Alex McFarland is an apologist/evangelist, author of eighteen books, and is host of the *Exploring the Word* live radio broadcast on American Family Radio. As an apologist/evangelist, Alex has been privileged to work with James Dobson and Focus on the Family, the North American Mission Board (NAMB), and many others. He has preached in all fifty states and internationally. Find him online at www.alexmcfarland.com.

Together Tony Beam and Alex McFarland lead the Center for Christian Worldview and Apologetics on the campus of North Greenville University. For more information about North Greenville, "where Christ makes the difference," visit www.ngu.edu.